1889

Front endsheet: Centennial poster; New-York Historical Society. Back endsheet: The bosses of the Senate; *Puck*. Front cover: Shoshoni Indians greeting President Arthur, Sidney Mayer Collection; Grover Cleveland, White House Historical Association; assassination of Garfield, *Harper's Weekly*; Mrs. Cleveland, The White House Collection. Back cover: Arthur cartoon, New-York Historical Society; 1888 campaign item, J. Doyle DeWitt Collection; President Garfield, Lawnfield, Mentor, Ohio; Mark Twain, University of California at Berkeley; frog statue, J. Doyle DeWitt Collection.

VOLUME

7

THE AMERICAN HERITAGE BOOK OF THE PRESIDENTS AND FAMOUS AMERICANS

★ ★ ★ ★ ★

JAMES ABRAM GARFIELD
CHESTER ALAN ARTHUR
GROVER CLEVELAND
BENJAMIN HARRISON

CREATED AND DESIGNED BY THE EDITORS OF
AMERICAN HERITAGE
The Magazine of History

12-VOLUME EDITION PUBLISHED BY
DELL PUBLISHING CO., INC., NEW YORK, N.Y.

LAWNFIELD, MENTOR, OHIO

James Abram Garfield

LIBRARY OF CONGRESS

Chester Alan Arthur

WHITE HOUSE HISTORICAL ASSOCIATION

Grover Cleveland

CINCINNATI HISTORICAL SOCIETY

Benjamin Harrison

 Library of Congress Catalogue Card Number: 67-12999.

CONTENTS
OF VOLUME SEVEN

FAMOUS AMERICANS

U.S. CAPITOL

THE TWENTIETH PRESIDENT (1881)

JAMES ABRAM GARFIELD

As a rule the American voter has preferred candidates of seeming straightforwardness and homely virtue to men of eloquence and elegance. The exceptions who did achieve high elective office, while they seasoned the nation's history with memorable oratory and their own personal color, did not often become President. Some tried futilely, among them Daniel Webster and silver-tongued William Jennings Bryan, but James A. Garfield, who did not try, succeeded.

Garfield's reputation as a debater and showman is not so great as those of Webster and Bryan. Yet he had been a preacher, an evangelist in fact, and his start in politics had been stimulated by an incident remarkably similar to the far more celebrated one—the Scopes trial of 1925—that closed Bryan's career.

In 1858 debate was probably America's most popular spectator sport. Although it was a year before publication of Darwin's *Origin of Species*, the ideas of evolution were in the air. A well-educated, thirty-seven-year-old Englishman named John Denton was touring the United States, proposing to debate all comers on the proposition: "Man, animals and vegetables came into existence by the operation of the laws of spontaneous generation and progressive development, and there is no evidence that there was ever any exercise of direct creative power on this planet." As Denton approached Ohio, it was reasonable that James A. Garfield, Disciple of Christ, should rise to the challenge.

Born in Cuyahoga County on November 19, 1831, Garfield had grown up in poverty on a farm. His father had died in 1833, and the children—James was the youngest of four—had to help their mother do a man's work. In 1848 the seventeen-year-old Garfield decided to go to sea: the best he could do was get a job on an Ohio canal, and the farthest he sailed was to Pittsburgh. Returning home later that year, he recuperated from an illness and the following

James Garfield, by C. Adele Fassett

The Union setback at the Battle of Chickamauga (above) on September 19, 1863, resulted in the discrediting of General William Rosecrans. But Major James Garfield distinguished himself as a quick-thinking leader.

spring began his formal education at a local denominational secondary school. In 1852 the Western Reserve Eclectic Institute (later Hiram College), where he had been a student for a term, gave him a job as a teacher; and by July, 1854, he had saved enough money to go to New England for a college education and was admitted to Williams College as a junior. At age twenty-four he returned to Ohio. His degree from an Eastern college made him a person of consequence, and in 1857 he became president of Hiram with its faculty of five. He was also an accomplished preacher whose sermons, delivered in a melodic, clear voice under the branches of Ohio trees, made the faithful feel—according to a friend's account—"as if they had been transplanted away from earth to some tranquil, beautiful region of heaven." His personal affairs were going as well as his professional ones: on November 11, 1858, he married Lucretia Rudolph, whom he had been courting since their childhood.

Thus equipped, the preacher-teacher and recent bridegroom prepared for John Denton. And prepare he did: unlike the debater's forty previous opponents, Garfield did not simply rehearse and solidify his own orthodox religious position; instead he read Denton's essays and book, studied biology, geology, and anthropology, and sent friends to take notes on Denton's debating technique.

Unfortunately, although Garfield's preparatory notes have been preserved, a record of the debate has not. It is known, however, that the Chagrin Falls hall, with its capacity of one thousand people, was filled for most of the five days of the debates and that John Denton, at the conclusion, acknowledged that Garfield was his strongest opponent to date. Garfield then made a well-received lecture tour of the state, speaking on "Geology and Religion." And in the spring of 1859, he turned his persuasiveness to different use and ran successfully for the Ohio senate.

Garfield was rapidly becoming Republican leader in the senate when the Civil War broke out and he became colonel of an Ohio regiment. As an officer, Garfield forged success from the same elements that had shaped his political career: he was part evangelist, part scholar. Having filled his regiment with enlistees stimulated by his florid oratory and stirring patriotism, he then had to learn what to do with his soldiers. After thoroughly studying the training manuals, he began to read accounts of famous battles and the tactics of Wellington and Napoleon. He constructed models and plotted his battles, using wooden blocks for men. In January, 1862, he led his men against a Confederate force, led by a West Pointer, at Middle Creek, Kentucky; his victory there was one of the few the Union could count at this stage of the war. Afterward he was promoted to brigadier general.

In September, 1862, the Ohio Republicans met in Garrettsville to select a candidate for the United States House of Representatives. Garfield, the only one of five hopefuls who was absent, was chosen, and for good reason: he was well educated, religious, well-known. Broad-shouldered, about six feet tall, and ruggedly handsome, he had the manners and personality to match his good looks, and he had demonstrated on the battlefield his ability to lead men and impress his colleagues. Garfield promised to return to the war even if elected to Congress, which he was.

C. C. TRAVIS COLLECTION

In early 1863, Congressman-elect Garfield reported as chief of staff to General W. S. Rosecrans, commander of the Army of the Cumberland. The two officers promptly established an affectionate rapport. In August, Rosecrans, against the advice of most of his officers, but with Garfield's approval, risked his strong position at Murfreesboro, Tennessee, by attempting to drive the Confederate forces under General Bragg from the state. During the engagement at Chickamauga in September, Rosecrans erred in reorganizing his lines, weakening the flanks and forcing his army to fight defensively. Garfield helped prevent a rout by riding along the front and acting as Rosecrans' eyes, but a Union victory was by this time out of the question. After the battle, both armies remained more or less as they had been. Rosecrans, however, was discredited.

The relative responsibility of Garfield and Rosecrans for the wasteful encounter has never been fully explained. When Garfield retired from the battlefield in December, 1863, and took his seat in Congress, he defended his former commander, but in later years was less willing to exonerate General Rosecrans. The general, too, vacillated between praise for and resentment toward his former staff officer. Many years later, when Garfield was being mentioned as a possible candidate for the Presidency, Rosecrans wrote: "When he [Garfield] came to my headquarters I must confess I had a prejudice against him, as I understood that he was a preacher who had gone into politics. . . . The more I saw of him the better I liked him. . . . His views were large and he was possessed of a thoroughly comprehensive mind." But when Garfield actually was the candidate, Rosecrans campaigned against him, claiming that "seventeen years is a long time, and many a splendid young man in less time has descended from honor to infamy."

Garfield, immediately placed on the Committee on Military Affairs, and later on the committees on Appropriations and on Ways and Means, rapidly orated his way to prominence in the House. An advocate of stern Reconstruction and conservative financial policies, he was not always in agreement with Lincoln; but although he was all but certain that General George McClellan, a Democrat, would win the presidential election of 1864, Garfield did not oppose Lincoln's renomination. Garfield was in the Exchange Building on New York's Wall Street when news of Lincoln's assassination reached the city. Outside the building an angry crowd assembled, ready to seek vengeance on the neighboring headquarters of the Democratic New York *World*. After a number of speakers tried without success to quiet the crowd, Garfield stepped out on a balcony. With scarcely fifty words, which rang out across the street, the former evangelist turned an ugly mob into a prayer meeting: "Fellow-citizens: Clouds and darkness are around about Him! His pavilion is dark waters and thick clouds of the skies! Justice and judgment are the establishment of his throne! Mercy and truth shall go before his face! Fellow-citizens: God reigns, and the Government at Washington still lives!"

The grandiloquent rhetoric of Garfield and the political expertise of Maine's James G. Blaine provided ideal support for House Republican leader Thaddeus Stevens. When Stevens retired in 1868, the two representatives became their party's congressional leaders. Temperamental opposites and not without their disagreements, Garfield and Blaine nevertheless made an effective team, providing leadership when President Grant provided none, working well enough together to maintain significant Republican strength even as the barren and stormy years of the Grant administration stimulated the resurrection of the Democratic party. The scandals of the General's Presidency touched both men, but as the administration approached its conclusion, both congressmen seemed to be emerging relatively unstained, and both began to feel the urge to move on to the Senate.

In 1876 Blaine sought and won Maine's senatorial seat. When the presidential election that year was thrown into the House, Garfield led the fight and framed the legislation that resulted in the election of Rutherford B. Hayes. The victory gave Garfield the opportunity to follow his old colleague, Blaine, into the Senate, for Hayes's appointment of Senator John Sherman of Ohio as Secretary of the Treasury vacated the seat that Garfield coveted. At this time, state legislatures still elected United States senators, and the Ohio legislature was dominated by a Republican majority. Garfield's record and his popularity—he had never been defeated in an election, even in recent years when Democrats had swept most offices in western Ohio—made him by far the strongest candidate. The new President, however, requested that he remain in the House, with its somewhat more frantic politics, where Garfield's legislative skills would do the administration the most good. The congressman agreed.

LIBRARY OF CONGRESS

This pro-Garfield print shows him cutting down weeds of corruption surrounding the White House.

In January, 1880, the Ohio legislature convened to elect a senator for the term beginning March 4 of the following year. Garfield, as House Minority Leader, had served the Hayes administration and his party faithfully, and now he wanted that Senate seat. With the support of Secretary Sherman, a candidate for his party's presidential nomination, the congressman was elected with ease. But Garfield's persistent desire to sit in the United States Senate was destined to be frustrated forever. A peculiar accident kept him from that chamber.

Garfield had in his eighteen congressional years earned a nationwide reputation. His election to the Senate was noted with approval throughout the nation: a Milwaukee newspaper commented that he "is exceptionally clean for a man who has been engaged for twenty years in active politics." As a national figure, he was naturally mentioned as a presidential candidate, but he apparently never took the possibility very seriously; besides, he firmly believed that no avowed candidate could win a nomination. Although he refused to seek the office and frequently alluded to his lack of qualifications for it, Garfield was not impervious to the reality that deadlocked conventions frequently turned to men of his mold when seeking a compromise candidate. He was aware that he might become President—but only accidentally. And the Republican party, fast losing the power it had held for two decades, was eminently accident-prone.

The party was divided into two factions: the "Stalwarts" and the "Half-Breeds." In truth there was but a shade of difference between them, although the former professed to be conservative and the latter, moderate. Led by Senator Roscoe Conkling of New York, the Stalwarts favored the nomination of former President Ulysses S. Grant, recently returned from a triumphant world tour. But the Half-Breeds favored the candidacy of their leader, James G. Blaine. Squeezing between the barely perceptible gap that separated the factions were several candidates, John Sherman being the strongest. Nominating Grant, Conkling announced that the election would determine whether the United States would be "republican or Cossack," and painted the General as the foe of "communism, lawlessness and disorder . . . charlatans, jayhawkers, tramps, and guerillas. . . ."

After a long and spirited demonstration that threatened to carry all the delegates in its swell, the former evangelist stepped forward to nominate Sherman. He remembered his old trade well: the convention quieted and was again transported—this time silently—by the musical voice that so eloquently called for "party harmony." Garfield could not secure Sherman's nomination, but he had stemmed the Grant tide, and after his speech the anti-Grant forces grew harmonious enough to make certain their actions would work against the General as well as for their candidates.

Grant consistently led the balloting with slightly over three hundred votes. But another Garfield coup—political, not verbal—had prevented the ex-President's nomination on the first ballot. The Stalwarts had placed a unit rule before the convention; if it had passed, each state would have had to cast all its votes for the candidate with the majority support. Only because of the successful efforts of the opposition, led by Garfield, was there any contest at all.

On the second day of balloting, Sherman telegraphed the convention, asking his supporters to vote for Garfield. When, on the thirty-fourth ballot, seventeen votes were cast for him, Garfield protested: "I rise to a point of order. No man has a right, without the consent of the person voted for, to announce that person's name and vote for him in this convention. Such consent I have not given." He was interrupted by the chairman; two ballots later he was the Republican presidential candidate. To appease the Stalwarts, the vice presidential nomination went to Conkling's associate, Chester A. Arthur of New York.

CULVER PICTURES

At the Republican convention of 1880 Stalwart Roscoe Conkling of New York, above, fought in vain to have ex-President Grant nominated a third time.

In the almost issueless campaign between Garfield and Winfield S. Hancock, the Democratic party was called "a party of famine . . . a good friend of early frost . . ." and the Republican candidate was accused of having an unpaid tailor's bill in Troy, New York. The Democrats did have one good charge to use against Garfield, but they failed to make the most of it.

One of the major scandals of the Grant administration had involved the government-subsidized Union Pacific Railroad, whose directors also controlled the Crédit Mobilier Company of America, which charged excessively high fees to the Union Pacific for railroad construction. Congressman Oakes Ames, one of the Crédit Mobilier directors, had a brilliant system for winning the support of his legislative colleagues in a way that did not on the surface appear corrupt. Garfield's involvement in the scheme was typical. In 1868 Ames told Garfield of a fine opportunity to buy some Crédit Mobilier stock; he need not decide then, Ames told him, for the stock would be put aside, on option. Thus Garfield neither bought the stock nor accepted it as a gift. Nevertheless, in June, 1868, he received a dividend check for $329. So during the election campaign of 1880, "three twenty-nine" became a Democratic war cry, and there was little Garfield could do about it.

During that same campaign, however, a letter was forged in Garfield's handwriting. In it, the Republican candidate stated that he favored unlimited importation of Chinese laborers. Calculated to lose him the labor vote, the letter contained two spelling errors, but since his spelling prowess was well-known, the forgery was exposed. The incident more than offset the Democrats' gains from the Crédit Mobilier affair.

Garfield won the presidential election by the comfortable electoral vote of 214 to 155, although he received fewer than ten thousand more votes than General Hancock in an election in which over nine million Americans voted.

No sooner had Garfield been inaugurated than the breach between the Stalwarts and the Half-Breeds reopened. The President's appointment of Blaine as Secretary of State infuriated the Stalwarts; and when William H. Robertson, a long-time antagonist of Conkling, was appointed collector of the Port of New York, thus challenging Conkling's control of patronage, the senator tried to block the appointment. Two days before Congress finally confirmed Robertson's position, Conkling and Thomas Platt, New York's junior senator, resigned. The state legislature failed to re-elect them when they asked Albany for vindication.

When Thomas L. James of New York was appointed Postmaster General, *The New York Times* was crusading for an investigation of what it called the Star Route Frauds. The Post Office Department had for years had huge deficits, and Congress, in passing the necessary appropriations, had assumed that the loss was due to the high cost of delivering mail in the rural West. The *Times* investigation revealed that thousands of dollars were being spent for deliveries to some places that received mail no more than three times a year. With President Garfield's approval and the help of Attorney General Wayne MacVeagh, James began a thorough and public investigation. It was found that under previous Republican administrations, contracts had been awarded to certain carriers closely associated with department administrators and Republican leaders. Although a number of high-ranking Republicans were implicated, Garfield, to his credit, instructed the Postmaster General to continue to release his findings. The scandal, which outlived Garfield, was a catalyst in the establishment of civil service reform.

On July 2, 1881, President Garfield left the White House for a trip to New England, where he intended to introduce his two sons to his alma mater, Williams College. In the Washington train station, a lawyer and disappointed office seeker named Charles J. Guiteau approached the President from behind, and while shouting, "I am a Stalwart and now Arthur is President!" fired two shots from a pistol. One bullet grazed Garfield's arm, but the other lodged in his back. He lay in the White House for two months while doctors weakened his condition by their futile and unsanitary attempts to locate and remove the bullet. Then he asked to be taken to the seaside, hoping that the ocean air would cure him.

The President remained conscious and reasonably alert during his illness. Once—but only once—he asked about Guiteau. "He must be insane," he judged. "Why should he want to kill me?" At Elberon, New Jersey, on September 19, 1881, James A. Garfield died.

—DAVID JACOBS

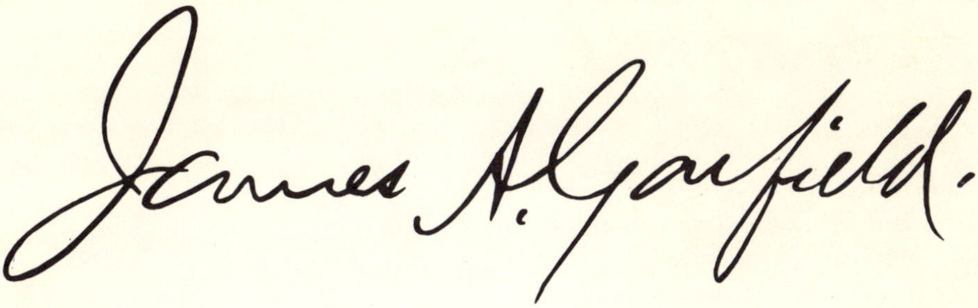

A PICTURE PORTFOLIO

LAWNFIELD, MENTOR, OHIO

This china pitcher commemorates the death of President James A. Garfield, who was shot by an assassin only four months after his inauguration in 1881.

MAN OF DESTINY

One does not seek office; the office must seek the man. To appear to conform with this mythical tradition was long considered requisite to success in American politics, and for many years most office seekers dutifully played the game of "hide-and-be-found." For James Abram Garfield, however, it was more than a game: because he had gained eminence through nonpolitical achievements, it was absolutely essential that he appear to be bound by destiny for high office. When he decided at the age of twenty-eight to enter politics, he was already well-known throughout Ohio as a former schoolteacher and college president and, especially, as the evangelist with the enchanting voice who had toured the state defending God and good against the heretical assault of an evolutionist. His mother cried when he confided his political ambitions; some friends thought it sacrilegious to turn his prestige as a preacher into a political tool. Clearly, the public could not be allowed to share this opinion. He could not enter politics; he would have to be transported in. So, as Garfield reclined beneath his halo, his good friend Harmon Austin did the work. At first skeptical of Garfield's decision, Austin nevertheless became his friend's lifetime political manager. He helped him win a seat in the state legislature in 1859 and three years later, with Garfield off fighting the Civil War, engineered Garfield's nomination to the House of Representatives. The illusion was perfectly drawn: the candidate was not present when nominated, hardly campaigned, and said that he would continue to serve in the Army if elected. But he won. And thus did office "seek" James A. Garfield.

BOTH: LAWNFIELD, MENTOR, OHIO

James Garfield and Lucretia Rudolph (above) were married in 1858. Twenty-two years later, when Garfield was a presidential candidate, the biographical comic strip opposite was published. Number 1 alludes to his role in the Crédit Mobilier scandal of 1873 and number 10 to another scandal of the Grant administration. But 4, 6, 7, and 9 are completely fictional: by the age of fourteen he had memorized several books; his father had died when James was not yet two years old; people were drawn to, not driven from, his preaching; and he did not leave the Army to campaign for Congress. (In fact he stayed in for almost a year after his election.)

NEW-YORK HISTORICAL SOCIETY

OFFICE OF "PUCK" 23 WARREN ST. NEW YORK.
MAYER, MERKEL & OTTMANN, LITHOG. 23-25 WARREN ST. N.Y.

PUCK'S LIFE OF GARFIELD.

WINFIELD SCOTT HANCOCK

General Winfield Scott Hancock, the Democrats' colorless presidential candidate in 1880, was described as "a good man, weighing 250 lbs. . . . with a record as stainless as his sword." Named for Winfield Scott, the famous general of the War of 1812, Hancock entered West Point at sixteen. Graduating in 1844, he served in the Mexican War, the Seminole War, and the Kansas Border War. As a major general in the Civil War, he commanded divisions in the battles of Fredericksburg and Chancellorsville and won particular distinction at Gettysburg, selecting the field of battle and repulsing repeated attacks by Lee. In 1868 his war record first brought him consideration for the Democratic nomination. When the party convened in Cincinnati twelve years later, Hancock—the man least likely to offend any of the various factions—was nominated for President. The campaign of 1880 was without major political issues, and both parties indulged in personal invective. Hancock was denounced as one who did "nothing but eat, drink, and enjoy himself sensually," but even his enemies could find little to exploit in his spotless past. Narrowly defeated by James Garfield, whose plurality was fewer than ten thousand votes, General Hancock resumed his military duties as commander of the Division of the Atlantic and of the Department of the East. Hancock died in 1886 on Governor's Island, New York.

A DEADLOCK BROKEN

The Republican convention of 1880 was a drawn-out, stormy affair in which several candidates tried independently to stop the nomination of ex-President Ulysses Grant. Although strong enough to do so, they were unable to agree on another nominee, and the convention was deadlocked for thirty-four ballots. Then Senator-elect James Garfield's name was presented, and on the thirty-sixth ballot he won the nomination. His first job was to heal the rift between the factions—a formidable task. The Half-Breeds (moderates) had managed to secure the adoption of a platform plank pledging civil service reform. Since political power at that time meant control of patronage, the machine-dominated Stalwarts (conservatives) opposed the plank. To pacify both sides Garfield pledged reform, but promised to make appointments in consultation with those "whose knowledge of the communities in which the duties are to be performed best qualifies them to aid in making the wisest choice." Then he embarked on a speaking tour, which turned out to be as successful as his earlier appearances as an evangelist. After an issueless campaign, he defeated Democrat General W. S. Hancock by an electoral vote of 214 to 155. But the election revealed a growing dissatisfaction with both major parties: Peter Cooper, the Greenback party candidate, had received only 80,000 votes in 1876, but this time well over three hundred thousand farmers and laborers cast their votes for the Greenback-Labor nominee, James B. Weaver.

J. DOYLE DEWITT COLLECTION

A hand and a cock formed the rather trite campaign symbol of General Winfield Hancock, Garfield's opponent in the election of 1880. The card above was printed by a Republican newspaper, which probably distributed campaign souvenirs to subscribers in both parties. In the Puck *cartoon below, titled "Rutherford's Legacy," outgoing President Hayes leaves his neglected child with Garfield.*

WESLEY DAY COLLECTION

MEN OF LETTERS

BROWN BROTHERS

HENRY WADSWORTH LONGFELLOW

"Longfellow," wrote a French critic in 1851, "seems to us to occupy the first place among the poets of his country." Born in Portland, Maine, in 1807, Henry Wadsworth Longfellow enjoyed enormous popularity during his lifetime. A professor at Bowdoin and Harvard from 1829 to 1854, he traveled widely abroad and made many friendships among the great artists of Europe and America. His first book of poetry, *Voices of the Night*, appeared in 1839, the same year as his romantic novel, *Hyperion*. Three years later he published two more volumes, *Ballads and Other Poems* and *Poems on Slavery*, the latter reflecting his indignation at the existence of slavery in a country "so loud about freedom as ours!" *The Song of Hiawatha* (1855) was acclaimed by the London *Spectator* as a poem "which will doubtless live as long as the English language." A man of great gentleness and refinement, Longfellow delighted in society, admired Old World culture, and lamented the want in the American character of "many of the more generous and lofty traits which ennoble humanity." Before his death he published some thirty-one volumes of poetry, plays, and prose, including *Evangeline* (1847), *The Courtship of Miles Standish* (1858), and a three-volume translation of Dante's *Divine Comedy*. Longfellow died in Cambridge, Massachusetts, in 1882.

MARK TWAIN PAPERS
UNIVERSITY OF CALIFORNIA AT BERKELEY

SAMUEL L. CLEMENS

Raised in the river town of Hannibal, Missouri, Samuel Langhorne Clemens had a carefree, rugged boyhood similar to that described in *The Adventures of Tom Sawyer* (1876) and *Adventures of Huckleberry Finn* (1885). Apprenticed to a printer as a youth, he traveled through the cities of the East and Middle West as a journeyman printer. From 1857 to 1861 he was a pilot on Mississippi steamboats, an experience he re-created colorfully in *Life on the Mississippi*, published in 1883. After a turn at prospecting in Nevada, he became a reporter, writing under the pseudonym "Mark Twain," the river term meaning two fathoms deep. Clemens moved to California in 1864 and won his first fame the next year when his short story *The Celebrated Jumping Frog of Calaveras County* was printed in newspapers across the country. In 1866 he began his long and successful lecturing career. His first important book, *The Innocents Abroad* (1869), was a satire based on his observations of American tourists in the Holy Land. *Roughing It*, an account of his Western experiences, followed in 1872 and another satire, *The Gilded Age*, in 1873. While his lectures and much of his writing reveal a robust frontier humor, his later works attest to his increasing bitterness. "Everything human is pathetic," he wrote toward the end of his life. "The secret source of humor is not joy but sorrow."

BROWN BROTHERS

HARVARD COLLEGE LIBRARY

WALT WHITMAN

"He was a genius," said a contemporary in describing the poet Walt Whitman, "who lived, apparently, in a world of his own." Nevertheless, Whitman represented himself in his poetry as the "average man." He extolled the uniqueness of the individual and the brotherhood of democracy. Whitman spent his early years in Long Island and Brooklyn, teaching school and pursuing a career in journalism. Between 1838 and 1848 he was associated with numerous magazines and newspapers, including the Democratic Brooklyn *Eagle*, which he edited for two years. In 1848 he spent three months in New Orleans, returned by way of St. Louis and Chicago, and shortly thereafter began work on the poems that appeared in 1855 in *Leaves of Grass*. Although Emerson praised it as "the most extraordinary piece of wit and wisdom that America has yet contributed," it was only after many successive revisions that the work received general acclaim. During the Civil War the poet worked as a volunteer nurse and a clerk in the Department of the Interior. Shortly after Lincoln's assassination he completed the poems in *Drum-Taps*, which included the moving "O Captain! My Captain!" His other collections include *Passage to India* and *Good-bye, My Fancy*. Whitman continued to publish until his death in 1892; his works reflect an optimistic faith in the American democracy.

HERMAN MELVILLE

Herman Melville was seventeen when he left his home in New York City in 1837 aboard a merchant ship bound for Liverpool. Four years later, with "an everlasting itch for things remote," he boarded the New Bedford whaler *Acushnet* and sailed to the South Pacific. Returning in 1844, he began re-creating his bizarre adventures in enduring prose. *Moby Dick*, his allegorical masterpiece about the pursuit of the great white whale, was gleaned from his eighteen months aboard the *Acushnet*; it was published in 1851. *Typee* (1846) and *Mardi* (1849) recall incidents of his capture by cannibals after deserting the whaler in the Marquesas Islands. *Omoo*, published in 1847, describes his subsequent life among the natives of Tahiti; and *White Jacket* (1850) is based on his return voyage to Boston aboard a Navy frigate. These novels—along with an early sea adventure, *Redburn* (1849), and the autobiographical *Pierre* (1852)—constituted the author's major published works until *Billy Budd* was printed posthumously in 1924. Melville had completed that superb short novel in 1891, the year of his death. Although he enjoyed a brief fame, he lived his later years in obscurity as a New York customs inspector, writing poetry in his free time. He was forgotten by his contemporaries; it was not until the 1920's that Americans rediscovered Melville's powerful prose.

BOTH: OHIO HISTORICAL SOCIETY

A NEEDLESS DEATH

As he was completing his fourth month in the Presidency, Garfield was being surreptitiously stalked by a pistol-bearing maniac named Charles J. Guiteau, a disappointed office seeker. The would-be assassin had his chance on an evening late in June when he found Garfield walking with James G. Blaine, but he lost his nerve. He recovered it, though, on July 2 in the Washington train station. Crying, "I am a Stalwart and now Arthur is President!" Guiteau fired twice, and one of the bullets penetrated the President's body. For two and a half months physicians tried to locate it. Actually—although the doctors could not have known it then—Garfield should have been up and around the whole time, regaining his strength. The bullet had lodged in his back muscles, just a few inches from the entry point, and his body had manufactured a protective cyst around it, rendering it harmless. But Garfield weakened and died, and Charles Guiteau was hanged for murder.

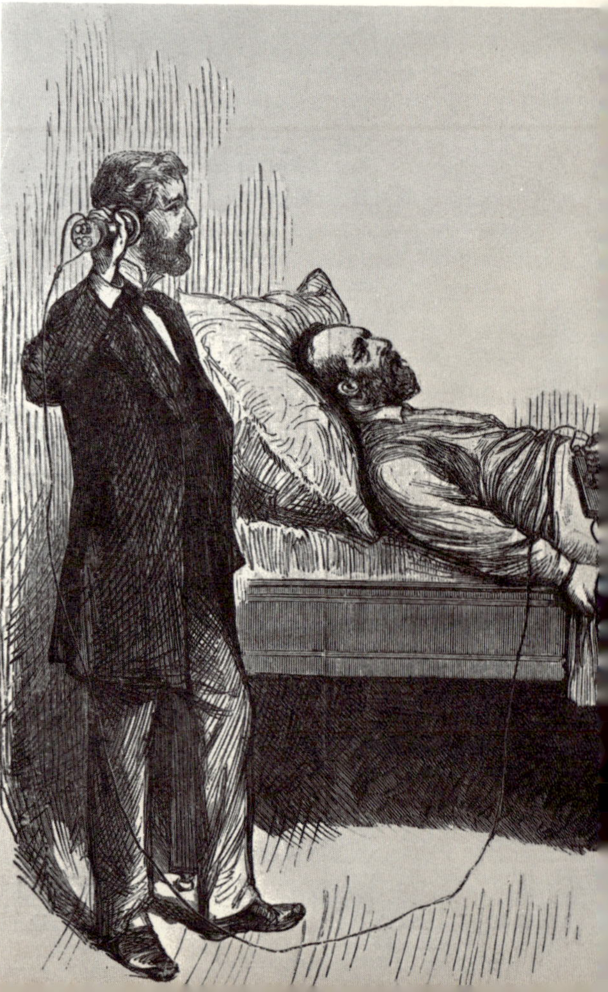

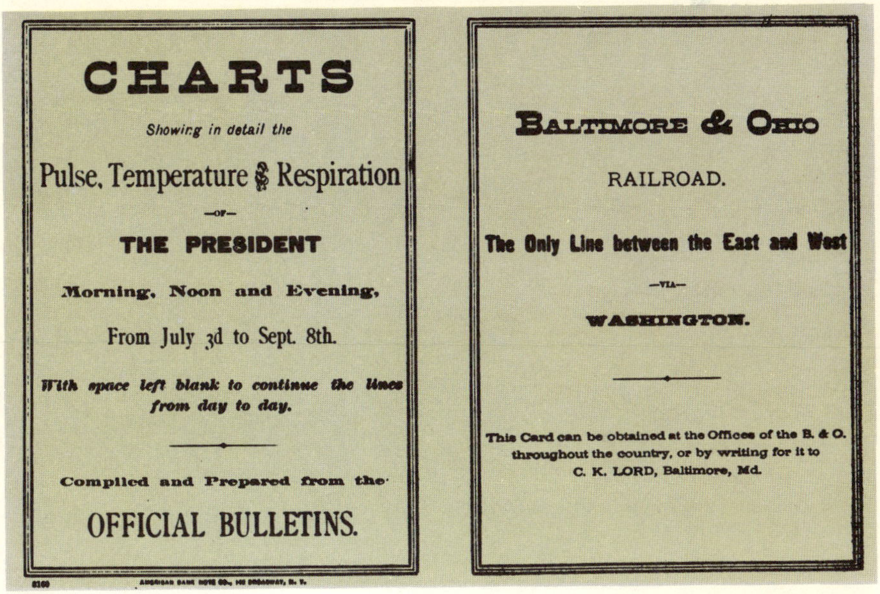
CHARTS
Showing in detail the
Pulse, Temperature & Respiration
—OF—
THE PRESIDENT
Morning, Noon and Evening,
From July 3d to Sept. 8th.
With space left blank to continue the lines from day to day.

Compiled and Prepared from the
OFFICIAL BULLETINS.

BALTIMORE & OHIO
RAILROAD.
The Only Line between the East and West
—VIA—
WASHINGTON.

This Card can be obtained at the Offices of the B. & O. throughout the country, or by writing for it to
C. K. LORD, Baltimore, Md.

WESTERN RESERVE HISTORICAL SOCIETY

"People must be tired of hearing of my symptoms," President Garfield said during the seventy-nine days he lay ill, alternately gaining and failing. Actually the public read every bulletin, eagerly seized every scrap of information; the Baltimore and Ohio Railroad even issued, free of charge, the progress chart above. On September 18, 1881, the exhausted President said with finality, "My work is done." He died the next night.

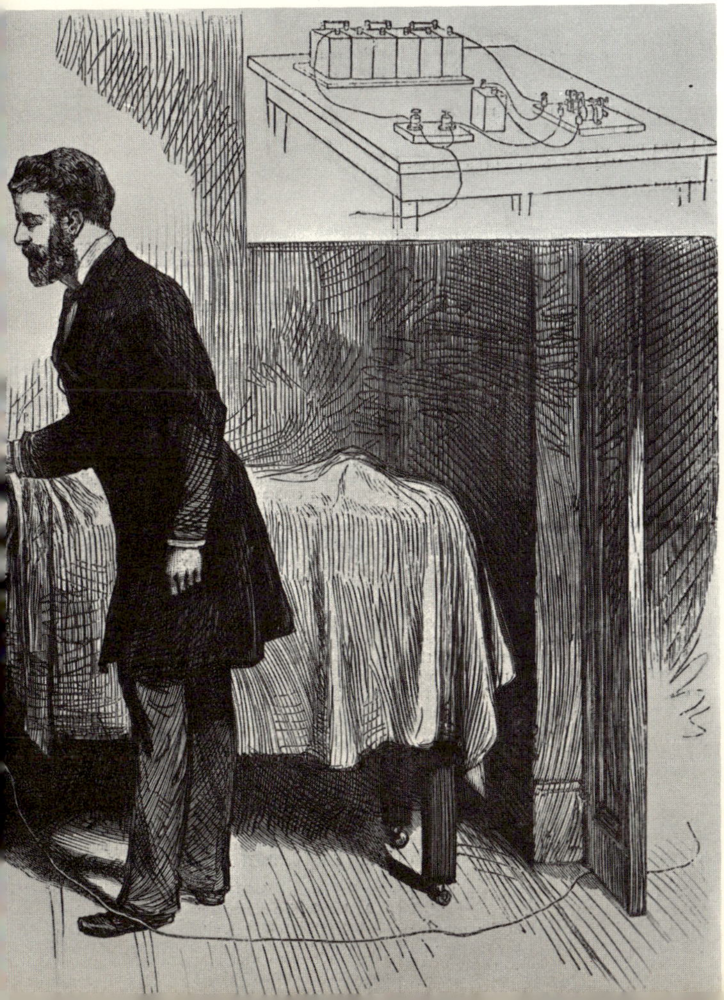

The President's doctors were baffled: Had the assassin's bullet lodged in Garfield's lung or liver or abdomen? They poked and probed and even asked Alexander Graham Bell to locate it with his electrical listening device (left) but without success. So they continued to probe, their unsterile instruments spreading infection throughout their patient's body, weakening him and causing his death. Ironically, the bullet need never have been removed.

FACTS IN SUMMARY: JAMES A. GARFIELD

CHRONOLOGY

UNITED STATES		GARFIELD
	1831	*Born November 19*
Van Buren elected President	1836	
Panic of 1837	1837	
Harrison elected President	1840	
Tyler becomes President	1841	
Polk elected President	1844	
Annexation of Texas	1845	
War with Mexico	1846	
Taylor inaugurated as President	1849	*Attends Geauga Academy*
Fillmore becomes President	1850	*Joins Disciples of Christ*
Compromise of 1850		
Clayton-Bulwer Treaty		
	1851	*Enters Western Reserve Eclectic Institute*
Pierce elected President	1852	
Kansas-Nebraska Act	1854	*Enters Williams College*
Republican party formed		
Civil war in Kansas	1856	*Graduates from Williams*
Buchanan inaugurated as President	1857	*Appointed president of Hiram College*
Dred Scott decision		
Lincoln-Douglas debates	1858	*Marries Lucretia Rudolph*
John Brown's raid at Harpers Ferry	1859	*Elected to Ohio senate*
Lincoln elected President	1860	
South Carolina secedes		
Fort Sumter fired upon	1861	*Commissioned lieutenant colonel in Ohio Volunteers*
First Battle of Bull Run		*Promoted to colonel*
Battle of Shiloh	1862	*Defeats Confederates at Middle Creek, Kentucky*
Monitor v. *Merrimac*		*Promoted to brigadier general*
Battle of Fredericksburg		*Commands brigade at Shiloh*
		Elected to U.S. House of Representatives
Emancipation Proclamation	1863	*Fights at Chickamauga*
Battle of Chancellorsville		*Begins term in Congress*
Vicksburg Campaign		
Battle of Gettysburg		
Lincoln re-elected President	1864	
Sherman's march to the sea		
Lee surrenders at Appomattox	1865	
Lincoln assassinated		
Johnson becomes President		

UNITED STATES March 4, 1881 — Sept. 19, 1881

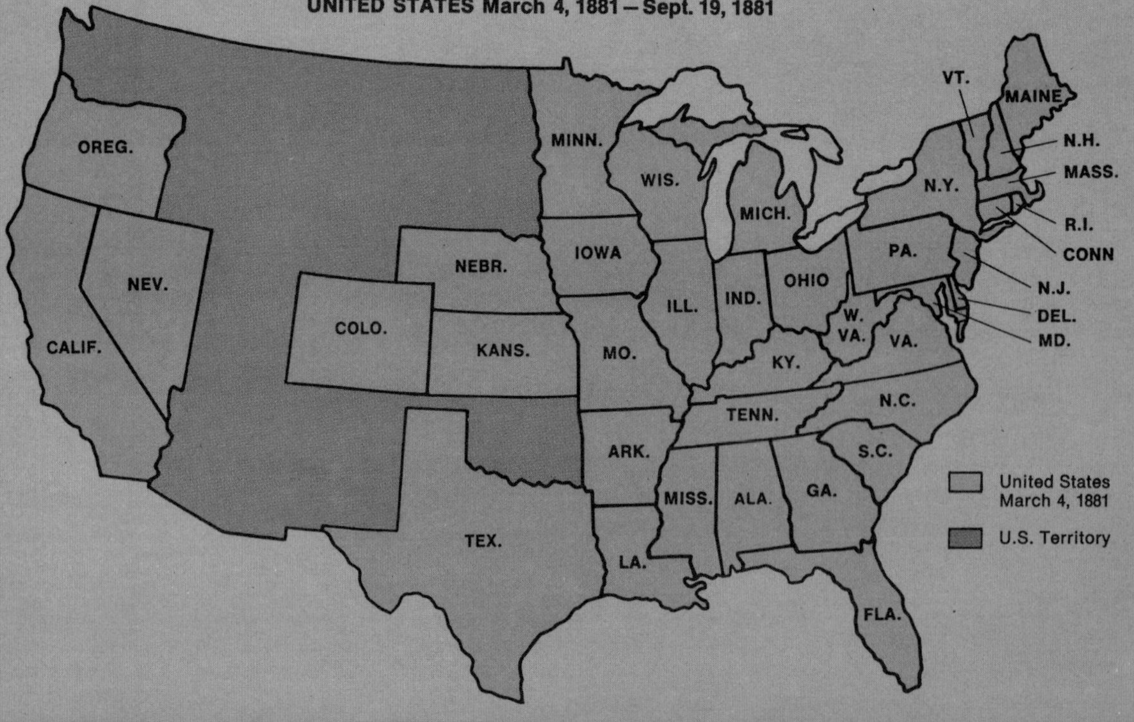

Civil Rights Act	1866	*Introduces bill to create a department of education*
Johnson impeached	1868	
Fourteenth Amendment ratified		
Grant elected President		
	1871	*Appointed chairman of House Committee on Appropriations*
Crédit Mobilier scandal	1872	
	1876	*Becomes Minority Leader in House*
Hayes elected President	1877	
Bland-Allison Act	1878	
	1880	*Elected to U.S. Senate*
		Elected President
Arthur becomes President	1881	*Approves investigation of "Star Route Frauds"*
		Shot by Charles Guiteau
		Dies of gunshot wound on September 19

LAWNFIELD, MENTOR, OHIO

This stained-glass memorial to Garfield is kept in a standing frame in the study of his home in Ohio.

BIOGRAPHICAL FACTS

BIRTH: Orange Township, Ohio, Nov. 19, 1831

ANCESTRY: English and French

FATHER: Abram Garfield; b. Worcester, N.Y., 1799; d. Orange Township, Ohio, 1833

FATHER'S OCCUPATION: Farmer

MOTHER: Eliza Ballou Garfield; b. Richmond, N.H., 1801; d. Mentor, Ohio, 1888

BROTHERS: Thomas (1822–?); James Ballou (1826–1829)

SISTERS: Mehitabel (1821–?); Mary (1824–1884)

WIFE: Lucretia Rudolph; b. Hiram, Ohio, April 19, 1832; d. Pasadena, Calif., March 14, 1918

MARRIAGE: Hiram, Ohio, Nov. 11, 1858

CHILDREN: Eliza Arabella (1860–1863); Harry Augustus (1863–1942); James Rudolph (1865–1950); Mary (1867–1947); Irvin McDowell (1870–1951); Abram (1872–1958); Edward (1874–1876)

EDUCATION: Attended Geauga Academy and Western Reserve Eclectic Institute; graduated (1856) from Williams College

HOME: Lawnfield, Mentor, Ohio

RELIGIOUS AFFILIATION: Disciples of Christ

OCCUPATIONS BEFORE PRESIDENCY: Schoolteacher; soldier; president of Hiram College

MILITARY SERVICE: Commissioned lt. col. of 42nd Ohio Volunteers in Aug., 1861; rose to brig. gen. of Volunteers (1862) and maj. gen. of Volunteers (1863)

PRE-PRESIDENTIAL OFFICES: Member of Ohio Senate; Member of U.S. House of Representatives; Chairman of House Committee on Appropriations; Minority Leader in U.S. House of Representatives

POLITICAL PARTY: Republican

AGE AT INAUGURATION: 49

DEATH: Elberon, N.J., Sept. 19, 1881

PLACE OF BURIAL: Lake View Cemetery, Cleveland, Ohio

ELECTION OF 1880

CANDIDATES	ELECTORAL VOTE	POPULAR VOTE
James A. Garfield Republican	214	4,453,295
Winfield S. Hancock Democratic	155	4,444,082
James B. Weaver Greenback–Labor	—	308,578
Neal Dow Prohibition	—	10,305

THE GARFIELD ADMINISTRATION

INAUGURATION: March 4, 1881; the Capitol, Washington, D.C.

VICE PRESIDENT: Chester A. Arthur

SECRETARY OF STATE: James G. Blaine

SECRETARY OF THE TREASURY: William Windom

SECRETARY OF WAR: Robert T. Lincoln

ATTORNEY GENERAL: Wayne MacVeagh

POSTMASTER GENERAL: Thomas L. James

SECRETARY OF THE NAVY: William H. Hunt

SECRETARY OF THE INTERIOR: Samuel J. Kirkwood

SUPREME COURT APPOINTMENT: Stanley Matthews (1881)

47th CONGRESS (March 4, 1881–March 4, 1883):
Senate: 37 Republicans; 37 Democrats; 1 Other
House: 147 Republicans; 135 Democrats; 11 Others

END OF PRESIDENTIAL TERM: September 19, 1881

THE TWENTY-FIRST PRESIDENT (1881–1885)

CHESTER ALAN ARTHUR

"The Gentleman Boss," Chester Alan Arthur, followed an unlikely road to the White House. But he certainly looked like a President—tall, stout, handsome, always nattily attired, "usually wearing," a contemporary Washingtonian observed, "a Prince Albert coat, buttoned closely in front, with a flower in the upper button-hole and the corner of a colored silk handkerchief visible from a side pocket."

Arthur's mother, Malvina Stone, was a frontier Vermonter; his father, William, born in Ireland, was a literate but feisty and foot-loose teacher who became a Baptist preacher, presiding over a succession of parishes in northern Vermont and upstate New York. Chester was born in 1830, but his birthplace is not definitely known. Some said that it was Fairfield, Vermont; others claimed that he came into the world in a log cabin at nearby Waterville; and during his Presidency some opponents stated, without proof, that he had actually been born in Canada and was therefore constitutionally ineligible to be President of the United States.

During the first nine years of his life, Arthur moved with his family five times, settling at last in Union Village, New York, where he attended the local school. Five years later, the Arthurs moved to Schenectady, and after an additional year of preparatory studies, Chester entered Union College there. He helped to pay his way through by teaching school and graduated, a member of Phi Beta Kappa, in 1848. He continued as a schoolmaster while studying law until 1853, when he moved to New York City for a year's polishing in the law office of a family friend. He was then admitted to the state bar. Though handsome, genteel, and well-read, Arthur was just another struggling young lawyer in the big city. In 1855 he argued one case of some importance, in which he represented a Negro woman who, because of her color, had been

President Arthur, as portrayed by Daniel Huntington

ejected from a streetcar in Brooklyn. He won $500 for his client and thereby earned for all Negroes better treatment on New York's public transportation. But, except for this case, Arthur's record was in no way distinguished.

Four years later he married a Virginia girl, Ellen Lewis Herndon, the daughter of a Navy hero. (She bore him three children—two of whom survived to adulthood—before she died of pneumonia in 1880.) Arthur joined the state militia, and he also entered politics. Because he helped return Edwin D. Morgan to a second term as governor of New York in 1860, Morgan made him a member of what was intended to be a purely ceremonial military staff. But when the Civil War began, Engineer in Chief Arthur was given additional duties as assistant quartermaster general and put in charge of feeding, housing, and equipping the thousands of war-bound soldiers pouring into New York City from all over the Northeast. The honesty and ingenuity he displayed in this job led to promotion to quartermaster general of the state; in December, 1863, a year after he retired (along with the outgoing Governor Morgan), his successor, a Democrat, noted admiringly that Arthur had saved the government much money and time by creating "a well-organized system of labor and accountability . . . at a period when everything was in confusion. . . ."

For Arthur the prestige of the position and the many new acquaintances it provided were pivotal; before the war was over he had become a prominent lawyer and was growing wealthy through his handling of war-claims cases. He knew that if he desired, he could rise in politics as well. But in the two and a half decades that followed the Civil War the major political parties were mercenary armies whose major functions were winning elections, getting jobs, and doing favors (for a consideration). One of the qualities that had set Chester Arthur apart was his complete honesty. He reconciled his standards with those that governed the political machine by approaching politics in the gentlemanly guise of a professional dilettante.

If he was going to play it as a game, he was at least in the big leagues: the American political machine had been invented, elaborated, and codified in New York State, which had produced the first boss—Alexander Hamilton—and some remarkably talented successors, such as Martin Van Buren and Thurlow Weed. A machine had to be thoroughly organized, from the local district on up, and had to be led by a strong man who derived his power from control over federal job appointments. At the time, there was no civil service as such; federal appointees were usually picked by and from the "in" party for services rendered at election time; often that was their only qualification for employment. In return, these party workers were expected to pay a percentage of their salaries into the party treasury and perform regular party duties. This method of hiring and firing was not productive of disinterested public service: federal jobholders put themselves and the party ahead of all other responsibilities. Bribery, graft, and thievery were common.

Into this world of high politics Chester Arthur now moved. He did so at a critical moment, for leadership of the state Republican party was in doubt. The old "conservative" leaders—Weed, William Seward, and former Governor Morgan—had remained loyal to Andrew Johnson, and the Radical landslide of 1866 had reduced their influence. But the Radicals were not yet well organized. In this intramural warfare, the newly elected United States senator, Roscoe Conkling, a flamboyant personality and an unforgettable orator, sought strength by wooing the conservative Republicans. This brought to his support Chester Arthur, who was by 1868 chairman of the state Republican executive committee and of the Central Grant Club of New York. The election of 1868 raised Grant to the Presidency, and the Conklingites became his favorites in New York: the New York machine became a Grant machine, nurtured by Grant patronage and controlled by Senator Conkling. For a while Arthur had only the kind of role he preferred—quiet organizer of party affairs.

But in 1871 Grant needed a man with a good reputation to take over the New York Custom House; his earlier appointee, Thomas Murphy, had been exposed as corrupt. So at the end of November, 1871, Chester Arthur reluctantly became collector for the Port of New York.

The custom house was the cornerstone of the machine. It employed over one thousand people, and the turnover when the White House changed hands was enormous: one party's hacks would trail out as another's trailed in. Arthur's supervision of this army and its nominal responsibilities for collecting customs duties was probably better than that of most of his predecessors. Certainly he remained above the sordidness himself. However, at the time he became collector, there was a growing movement for reform of the bureaucracy; the machines and the patronage concept were under fire.

As part of a national reaction to the Grant scandals, a Democratic administration was voted into power in New York State in 1874. Once the Conkling organization failed to hold the state for the Republican party, it was in danger. Reverse followed reverse, and by 1876 the tide was running heavily against the machine. The reformers now felt strong enough to strike at its roots—the custom house. Soon after Hayes came into office in 1877, an investigation was begun. At the time it was not aimed at Arthur; there was general agreement that he had done a good job, although he had clearly allowed the custom house payroll to grow too long. But as the investigation progressed, the politicians who saw the situation as an opportunity to ruin Conkling built a case for removing Arthur and one of his deputies, Alonzo Cornell. The custom house was shown (to no one's surprise) to be tarnished by fraud and inefficiency. Hayes issued an order forbidding government employees to engage actively in partisan politics, and when Arthur and Cornell did not comply with the demand, the administration, in September of 1877, revealed plans for changes of leadership at the Port of New York. For a while the Senate sustained Conkling in his opposition, but by the following July, Arthur and Cornell were forced to step down.

Puck

Hayes fired Arthur and Cornell from the New York Custom House partly to weaken Senator Conkling's machine. When Conkling won a third term in 1879, Puck *saw it as a renewal of the reformers' burdens.*

The machine, however, was not wrecked yet. Helped by a national issue—Southern exclusion of Negroes from voting—it pulled the state Republicans together to nominate and elect Cornell as governor in 1879. Roscoe Conkling was re-elected to the Senate. And as 1880 approached, the machine began to work for the nomination of Ulysses S. Grant for a third term.

But the Conklingites and the rest of the old-line "Stalwart" allies fell about ninety votes short of success at the convention. Their opponents managed on the thirty-sixth ballot to unite on reformer James A. Garfield of Ohio. The natural inclination of the delegates was to pull the party together for the campaign by choosing a Stalwart from New York as the vice presidential candidate. Levi P. Morton was asked to accept second place, but refused on the advice of Conkling, furious that Grant had not been chosen, and Massachusetts boss George Boutwell. Then the New. York delegation took matters into its own hands, informing the Ohio delegation that Chester Arthur would be the state's choice. Ohio, in turn, approached Arthur, who hastened to discuss the matter with Conkling. During a stormy interview, Conkling urged Arthur to drop the offer "as you would a red-hot shoe from the forge." But now Arthur realized that he wanted the nomination. "This trickster of Mentor [Garfield]" might well be "defeated before the country," as Conkling was angrily predicting. Nevertheless, Arthur told him, "The office of Vice President is a greater honor than I ever dreamed of attaining. [Indeed, it would be the first time Arthur stood for election to any public office.] A barren nomination would be a great honor. In a calmer moment you will look at this differently." Conkling thought not and warned him to "contemptuously decline it."

"Senator Conkling," said Arthur evenly, "I shall accept . . . and I shall carry with me the majority of the delegation." Conkling stormed out of the room. Arthur was nominated on the first ballot.

Politically defensible, the nomination nonetheless sent a shudder through liberal Republican ranks. The Republican platform included a reform plank. Arthur had been fired recently by a Republican President under circumstances that associated him with corruption, and he was a henchman of Conk-

SIDNEY MAYER COLLECTION

The elegant Arthur was appalled at the style of the furnishings that had been gathered in the White House over the years. He refused to move in until twenty-four wagonloads of decorations and furniture, some of it priceless, had been auctioned off and the Mansion completely redone in late-Victorian style (above).

ling's, the man who sneered at a reformed bureaucracy as the "snivel service." What else could be said about him? He was a party committeeman, a back-room operator. He was pleasant and well-mannered enough, and he was known as a first-class fisherman; he could quote from Burns in an amazingly perfect Scottish accent, and he knew how to live graciously. But he had no national reputation save what stemmed from his contretemps with the reformers. To some it seemed that Conkling must have engineered the nomination to wreck the ticket. Readers of the *Nation* who wanted to vote for Garfield wrote to ask if they could do so without also voting for Arthur. Editor E. L. Godkin replied that they could not, but that it did not really matter. "There is no place in which his powers of mischief will be so small as in the Vice Presidency. . ." Godkin wrote. "It is true General Garfield . . . may die during his term of office, but this is too unlikely a contingency to be worth making extraordinary provision for."

In the early months of the campaign Arthur surprised the voters by endorsing in his Letter of Acceptance civil service reform. Even some of his critics felt his letter was better than Garfield's. On the other hand, Garfield would have to assure the Conkling machine of fair treatment in return for dedicated campaigning: New York was a key state. Republican strategists figured on a solidly Democratic South, and if New York and Indiana fell into the Democratic column too, Garfield would be beaten. It was therefore crucial that the New York organization put its whole heart and soul into the canvass. Arthur and Conkling played a waiting game and went off fishing. Finally, in August, Garfield was compelled to come east to deal with the Stalwarts; when he left they felt they had won all the concessions they wanted: the right to name the Secretary of the Treasury in Garfield's Cabinet and control over New York patronage. Garfield, however, believed he had involved himself in "no trades, no shackles"—promising only to discuss the New York appointments with Senator Conkling and the Stalwarts.

The wide divergency in their understanding began to be evident soon after Garfield was elected, with New York going Republican by 21,000 votes. The Stalwarts wanted Levi Morton for the Treasury post; Garfield denied he had ever made a promise about it. He offered to make Morton Secretary of the Navy, but Conkling would not budge. In the end the Cabinet did contain a man from New York, but it was Thomas L. James as Postmaster General.

Even before the inauguration Arthur dissipated the improvement in his public image that he had earned by his Letter of Acceptance: he was seen in Albany vigorously lobbying for the election of a candidate for the United States Senate, an activity that was considered unbecoming to a Vice President-elect. Then, at a testimonial dinner for Stephen Dorsey—who had managed the Republican victory in Indiana—Arthur was, to say the least, tactless and indiscreet. While praising Dorsey he spoke slyly of "the secrets of the campaign." Indiana, he noted, was normally Democratic, but "had been put down on the books" as a state the Republicans might carry "by close and perfect organization and a great deal of—." Here he paused, while knowing laughter burst from his audience along with cries of "Soap! Soap!"—the code word the Republicans had used in telegrams during the campaign when they meant "money." The implication was that the Indiana election had been bought. That kind of inside joke was fine for the drawing room, where Chester Arthur was at his best, but in these circumstances, with reporters listening to his speech, it did him a great deal of harm.

As Vice President, Arthur still demonstrated a lack of respect for his new position. Garfield, trying to keep the Stalwarts, the independents, and the "Half-Breeds" of James G. Blaine all happy, allowed himself to be guided on certain New York appointments by Conkling. But under pressure from Blaine and others to avoid the appearance of domination by "Lord Roscoe," Garfield suddenly named Conkling's leading reform antagonist, William H. Robertson, collec-

The bearded Charles Guiteau (on the witness stand in court, at right) joined with local and federal authorities to turn his trial for the murder of President Garfield into a farce. The police guard of the prisoner was lax; at far right, one of several unsuccessful attempts on his life is depicted. Reported Harper's Weekly: *"A reckless man, mounted on a fleet horse, was allowed to follow the prison van for more than half a mile, approach it, locate his victim, and then fire at him. . . . That the national government, in its own capital . . . should be unable to reserve to its own agencies the punishment of the murderer of the Chief Executive is something intolerable." Guiteau, convicted of murder, was executed on June 30, 1882.*

tor of the Port of New York. The fat was in the fire. At stake was not just the collectorship, but control of the state party, with Robertson building political strength at Conkling's expense. Conkling fought the nomination in the Senate, where the other members were inclined to support him; the old policy of senatorial courtesy, or control over local jobs, was on the line. Conkling, junior Senator Thomas C. Platt, Postmaster General James, and Vice President Arthur sent a letter of protest to Garfield. Arthur tried in private conversations to change the President's mind and in public made no secret of his opposition. Garfield was unmoved. He forced the Senate (which would have preferred to wait awhile in hopes that the crisis would go away) to choose between his wishes and those of Conkling. Conkling, who knew he would be defeated, resigned from the Senate, followed by Platt; they planned to return to Albany, expecting vindication through re-election. Robertson's appointment was quickly confirmed by the Upper House.

Vice President Arthur then hurried to the New York capital to labor in the cause of Conkling and Platt. If his politicking before the inauguration had raised some eyebrows, at this point it occasioned disgust. In Albany the ex-senators and the Vice President found that there would be no vindication; the machine had fallen apart under the stresses of individual ambitions and Conkling's loss of control in Washington. First to fall was Thomas Platt, who was careless enough to be caught *flagrante delicto* with a woman not his wife by a gang of political enemies. As the story was snickered through Albany, Platt decided he had best withdraw from the race. On July 1, 1881, Arthur thus lost one of his candidates, under the most humiliating of circumstances. The next day's events would make defeat of Roscoe Conkling inevitable.

On July 2, Garfield was shot by Charles Guiteau, a Stalwart, who declared he had shot Garfield to make Arthur President and end the quarrels over spoils. Under the darkest of clouds, Arthur left Conkling in New York and hurried to Washington; it was thought at first that the President would die within hours or days. When Garfield was said to be out of danger, Arthur returned to his New York City home for many weeks of seclusion. Government ground to a virtual halt, crippled by the incapacity of its Executive. Talk began to circulate that Arthur might have to step in as substitute, but the constitutional problem caused by Tyler's precedent—could a Vice President merely substitute for an ill President and then hand back the powers and duties when the President recovered, or was he required to *become* President?—was too great a stumbling block. Queried on the matter, Arthur flatly refused to take over. The weeks dragged on. Arthur's anxiety depleted his strength and his sense

BOTH: *Harper's Weekly*

of self-possession, so much so that confidants were seriously worried about his health. But the calmness and dignity with which he comported himself in public impressed everyone. When Garfield finally died, an acquaintance said, "Chet Arthur, President of the United States! Good God!" But by that time, the country as a whole was ready to accept Arthur as President, at least on a trial basis.

After taking the oath of office in New York on September 19, 1881, he tried to cope with a frightening situation he had helped create: because of a Democratic majority in the Senate (due to the resignations of Conkling and Platt), he had refused to step down as presiding officer to allow the election of a Senate president pro tempore before adjournment. So there was no one in the line of succession behind him. Supposing he were assassinated or died in a train wreck on his way to the Capital? He sent a letter, addressed to "The President," calling the Congress into emergency session; someone would open it if the tragedy occurred. Then he left for Washington.

As he assumed the Presidency, Arthur was confronted by a number of serious problems. First, he had to assure the country that he would not make Conkling, as some feared, "the power behind the throne." At the same time he had to create his own administration with men he got along with. He had a narrow line to walk. He also had to prosecute the trial of Guiteau. The Star Route mail frauds, uncovered while Garfield was in office, had to be dealt with. The cries for civil service reform, all the louder now because of Garfield's death, had to be listened to. There was a large and troublesome surplus in the Treasury, which was connected with a demand for reform of tariff schedules.

All told, Arthur did an acceptable job. Gradually the administration developed a definite Stalwart tinge, but at the same time Arthur tried to satisfy the other factions within the party in order to unify it. Conkling was kept at arm's length and so, increasingly, was the old Stalwart figurehead, U. S. Grant. Guiteau was brought to trial—albeit a sensational, ludicrous trial—found guilty, and hanged. And although it caused a great deal of embarrassment to the party in general and to the Stalwarts in particular, Arthur pressed the case against those responsible for the Post Office frauds. Among them were Stephen Dorsey and Thomas J. Brady, another party leader whom Grant had appointed second assistant postmaster general. Arthur was apparently sincere in his desire for convictions in the case, for he assigned two Democrats to handle much of the work and encouraged the Attorney General to prosecute the case "with the utmost vigor of the law." But there were many legal setbacks for the government, and eventually the two accused officials were adjudged legally innocent.

In civil service reform the President was more successful, even though it seemed that the Republican machine politicians would be able to block him. Arthur demanded reform in his first annual message; when Congress ignored his request, the voters seconded him by overturning the Republican control of the House in the mid-term elections. In his second annual message Arthur again called on the Congress to act, and the Pendleton bill was passed and was signed into law in January, 1883. The Civil Service Commission, created by the law, gradually brought one-tenth of government jobs under its supervision. Examinations were made prerequisites for employment, and penalties were set up for officials who demanded salary kickbacks. The commission praised the President for his support.

One notable temptation to bad government was provided by the Treasury surplus, which amounted to some eighty to one hundred million dollars a year. Resulting from high tariff revenues and taxes, the surplus money was, in effect, being taken out of circulation, and government spending was the only way of getting it back into the economy. Thus the politicians could justify legislation that had as its main purpose the gratification of their constituents: bills for pensions, bills for local public works. The Forty-seventh Congress requested, for instance, Arthur's signature on an appropriation of more than $18,700,000 to be spent on rivers and harbors; Arthur wanted to cut the surplus, but not by rash spending, and he vetoed the bill. (It was quickly passed over his veto.) He thought there were several better ways of dealing with the extra money: taxes and tariffs could be lowered and money could be spent on defense and reduction of the national debt. While on the one hand espousing a stringent economy in government, Arthur tried to put these alternatives into effective operation.

A tax relief act sponsored by Arthur achieved little. His tariff commission proposed downward revision of import duties, but Congress, goaded on by lobbies for various interests, tore the bill to pieces. A program of reciprocal trade treaties with other nations, which would have eliminated certain tariffs, did not win sufficient support. Arthur also tried to improve the military establishment, particularly the outdated Navy, but a combination of hurried planning by the administration and foot-dragging by the Democratic House limited the results. It was in reducing the public debt—by more than $400,000,000—that Arthur most effectively coped with the surplus, although he eliminated neither it nor its causes.

Perhaps, in the light of how Arthur achieved the Presidency, the most important characteristic of his administration was its tone. ". . . He acted from the start with remarkable tact and grace," commented Matthew Josephson, historian of the Age of Spoils. "In some ways he impressed . . . important businessmen especially as the most effective President since Lincoln"—even though he fell short of attaining many of his goals. And he impressed liberals as well as conservatives. "I can hardly imagine how he could have done better," said Henry Ward Beecher.

But his administration was far from a political success. He was unable to pacify the feuding factions in the party. And he refused to reconstruct the shattered Conkling machine in New York through the judicious use of patronage; he would not even remove Robertson from the New York collectorship. He made Conkling so angry that in the spring of 1883 his former mentor declared, "I have but one annoyance with the Administration of President Arthur, and that is, that, in contrast with it, the Administration of Hayes becomes respectable, if not heroic."

Without a strong party faction behind him, Arthur was unable to win a nomination for a presidential term in his own right in 1884, and the following year he even failed to receive a nomination from New York Republicans for a seat in the United States Senate. Exhausted by the strain of office, Chester Arthur died only twenty months after leaving the White House.

—MICHAEL HARWOOD

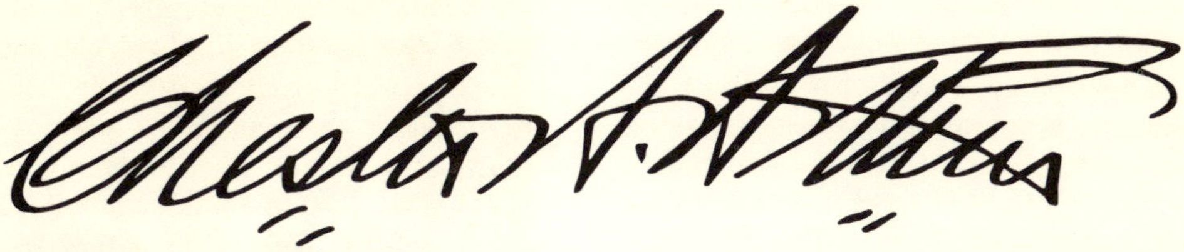

A PICTURE PORTFOLIO

CULVER PICTURES

Chester Arthur (depicted in a Puck *cartoon, above) had to deal with serious schisms in the Republican party during his forty-one and a half months as the President of the United States.*

For much of 1881 the nation suffered from the flaws of its system for presidential succession. Garfield (shown with Arthur on the flag at right) lay desperately ill for most of the summer, and because of the Constitution's uncertain phraseology on the matter, the Vice President was unable to take over the reins of government until the Chief Executive died. And for the first three weeks of Arthur's Presidency (he was sworn in by Justice John Brady in New York, below), there was no one behind him in the line of succession, since he and the Republicans in the Upper House had successfully prevented the Democrat-controlled Senate from electing a president pro tempore in its previous session.

J. DOYLE-DEWITT COLLECTION

LIBRARY OF CONGRESS

The cartoon at right, drawn by Joseph Keppler after Arthur became President, refers to the ending of King Henry IV, Part Two, *in which Falstaff assumes that the ascension of Prince Hal to the throne will not change their relationship. His royal friend responds, "I know thee not, old man . . . I have turned away from my former self; So will I those that kept me company." In most respects Keppler's wish came true. Arthur kept Roscoe Conkling out of White House councils, and when he offered a seat on the Supreme Court to the former senator from New York, Conkling, hurt, rejected it.*

NEW-YORK HISTORICAL SOCIETY

A FEARFUL NATION

"We learned of the shooting [of Garfield]," wrote a friend to former Secretary of the Treasury John Sherman, ". . . by a special telegram received on the train; and the first remark I heard was from a one-legged soldier, a major, who said: 'I fear that is done to make Arthur President and Conkling Premier Primate of the whole country. . . .' Then we had not even seen the telegram, and of course not the *printed* dispatches giving the words of the assassin at the time ['I am a Stalwart and now Arthur is President!']. . . . How fatal a mistake was made at Chicago in the nomination for the second place. The prayer for poor Garfield is *universal*. There is not popular confidence in the possible succession. . . ." The nation had good reason for its apprehension: Arthur had long been a tool of boss Roscoe Conkling and was apparently nothing but a spoilsman. But the Stalwarts, who must have secretly rejoiced when President Garfield died at last, and the rest of their countrymen were in for a surprise. Chester Alan Arthur filled his new role with dignity, honesty, and ability.

A GRAND SHAKESPERIAN REVIVAL.
(Which We Have But Little Hope of Seeing on the Stage of the National Capital.)

WESTWARD HO!

As have many Presidents, Chester Arthur found his labors and responsibilities exhausting. When he could, he took time off for trips—the most notable of which occurred in the summer of 1883. Accompanied by a few cronies, plus Lieutenant General Philip Sheridan, other high-ranking officers, seventy-five cavalry troopers, Indian guides, a photographer, and 175 pack animals, the President rode through western Wyoming to Yellowstone National Park. No reporters were included in the party, a fact that did not improve Arthur's relations with the fourth estate. He fished, watched Indian ceremonies, and accepted a pinto pony for his daughter, Nell, from the old Shoshoni chief Washakie. The vacation, which proved a tonic for the weary Chief Executive, is commemorated by a Wyoming mountain named Arthur Peak.

LIBRARY OF CONGRESS

Arthur was considered to be one of the finest fishermen in the country, adept at hooking large trout, salmon, and striped bass. One day off the coast of Rhode Island he hauled in an eighty-pound bass, said to be the biggest seen in those parts for many seasons. Above, the President poses for a camera before pushing off for a few hours of fresh-water bass fishing at Alexandria Bay, on the boundary between New York and Canada.

Frontier photographer F. Jay Haynes recorded Arthur's trip to Wyoming. At left are the Shoshoni Indians who welcomed the presidential party to Fort Washakie. The umbrellas that some of them carry are symbols of leadership.

Looking like characters out of a Gilbert and Sullivan operetta, Arthur and a few of his fellow campers (below) lounge around a midday repast on the trail. Arthur is seated in a camp chair at the center of the photograph. Among the other identifiable lunchers is General Philip Sheridan, resting second from left in the foreground. The gentleman between Sheridan and Arthur is probably Secretary of War Robert T. Lincoln, son of the late President.

BOTH: SIDNEY MAYER COLLECTION

STRONG-WILLED LADIES

ELIZABETH CADY STANTON

When Elizabeth Cady married Henry B. Stanton in 1840, she insisted that the word "obey" be stricken from the ceremony. Already interested in such reforms as temperance and abolition, Elizabeth Cady Stanton became a pioneer in the women's movement for equal rights. Attending an antislavery convention in London with her husband in 1840, Mrs. Stanton became acquainted with Lucretia C. Mott. When Mrs. Mott and other American women delegates were refused recognition because of their sex, Mrs. Stanton joined with them in planning a women's rights convention. Held in Seneca Falls, New York, in 1848, the meeting formally launched the feminist movement in the United States. Working closely with Susan B. Anthony, she planned campaigns and lecture tours and became president of the National Woman Suffrage Association in 1869. She was coeditor of the feminist weekly *Revolution* for two years and coauthor with Miss Anthony of the *History of Woman Suffrage*, published in the eighteen-eighties. A small woman of pleasing expression and snow-white hair at middle age, she spoke and wrote with an eloquence and persuasiveness that brought her respect even as a champion of an unpopular cause. She contributed many articles to newspapers and magazines and published her reminiscences, *Eighty Years and More*, in 1898.

CLARA BARTON

Clara Barton, founder of the American Red Cross, was a woman of great energy, initiative, and independence. A dedicated educator for eighteen years, she quit her profession in 1854 when she was superseded by a male principal in a New Jersey public school. Securing work in the Patent Office in Washington, she was in the Capital at the outbreak of the Civil War. Independent of any existing agency, she began organizing supply and nursing services for wounded Union soldiers, going onto the battlefields to oversee the operations. After the war she directed a four-year search for missing soldiers. Going abroad for her health in 1869, she became active in the International Red Cross of Geneva during the Franco-Prussian War, and on her return she worked to establish a similar institution in this country. In 1881 the American Red Cross was organized, and Clara Barton served as its president until 1904. It was largely through her efforts, also, that President Arthur secured adoption of the Geneva Convention in 1882 and that the "American Amendment," stipulating Red Cross relief in peacetime calamities as well as in war, was introduced at the International Red Cross Convention in 1884. Indefatigable in the alleviation of suffering, she directed the activities of the American Red Cross until her retirement at eighty-three. Clara Barton died in Maryland in 1912.

SUSAN B. ANTHONY

Devoted to social reform in general and woman suffrage in particular, Susan B. Anthony once said that she "would ignore all law to help the slave" and "ignore it all to protect an enslaved woman." Susan was a strong-willed, precocious child of Quaker background, who learned to read and write at the age of three. Like many women reformers of her day, she began her career as a teacher. At her home in Rochester, New York, she came in contact with such notable reformers as William Lloyd Garrison and William Ellery Channing and formed a lasting alliance with feminist Elizabeth Cady Stanton. Taking up the temperance movement, she helped to organize the first women's temperance society in 1852; she was also among the first to advocate Negro suffrage and unsuccessfully attempted to extend the franchise to women through the Fourteenth Amendment. Concentrating on women's rights, she helped to found the National Woman Suffrage Association in 1869 and served as president of its successor organization from 1892 to 1900. Opposition to the movement was widespread: in 1872 she was arrested and fined for voting in an election, and her lecture tours were often met with taunts, jeers, and flying objects. Undaunted, she continued her campaign, and before her death in 1906 she had won the battle for equal rights for women in four states.

ALL: LIBRARY OF CONGRESS

DOROTHEA DIX

"I have no particular love for my species," maintained humanitarian Dorothea Dix, "but own to an exhaustless fund of compassion." An intelligent and independent girl, Dorothea was only fourteen when she began teaching and nineteen when she opened a girls' school at the Dix mansion in Boston. Plagued by nerves and ill health, she left the school in 1835 and spent several months convalescing in England. After her return to Boston, she visited a nearby jail in 1841. Appalled at finding insane people locked up like thieves, she began her lifework of reform in the treatment of the mentally ill. Conducting an independent investigation of the state's prisons and almshouses, she reported to the Massachusetts legislature in 1843 the barbaric conditions under which the insane were herded together like animals, "*chained, naked, beaten with rods*, and *lashed* into obedience!" Continuing her investigations nationwide, she aroused public opinion and shocked state legislatures into action. Between 1841 and 1857 she was responsible for the founding or enlargement of hospitals for the mentally ill in sixteen states, Canada, England, and Italy. This heroic feat accomplished, she volunteered her services to the Union forces during the Civil War and was made superintendent of women nurses. Active in reform until her eightieth year, Dorothea Dix died in 1887.

AN HONEST LOSER

Although he proved to be an honest President (standing for reform of the civil service and against pork-barrel appropriation bills), Chester Arthur failed at that part of the political game that he might have been expected to master: he was unable to weld the Republican party together under his leadership. On the one hand, he attempted to steer a middle course between the opposing factions, being conciliatory toward each of them. This infuriated his friends the Stalwarts. On the other hand, in New York State he forced the party to nominate his Secretary of the Treasury, Charles J. Folger, for governor in 1882 rather than the incumbent Republican, Alonzo B. Cornell. The New York Republicans were so disrupted that many stayed away from the polls that fall, and an obscure Democratic mayor of Buffalo named Grover Cleveland won the governorship. The lack of a firm footing either in New York or within a particular faction of the party, plus the general Republican losses in the mid-term elections around the country, boded ill for Arthur's hopes of being elected to a presidential term of his own. But although he had little support within his party, he was a popular Chief Executive, perhaps because the voters were relieved to have their early fears of his honesty dispelled. Said Mark Twain, "I am but one in 55,000,000; still, in the opinion of this one-fifty-five-millionth of the country's population, it would be hard to better President Arthur's Administration. But don't decide until you hear from the rest." The rest got no chance to express their opinion of Arthur; at the 1884 convention the Republicans chose James G. Blaine to oppose Cleveland and thereby lost control of the White House.

The Democrats had long been crying that it was time to throw the rascals out; government needed a good house cleaning. In the Puck *cartoon (right) they look particularly dejected as they see their entry to the Capital city blocked by Arthur's support of the merit system in civil service employment.*

WESLEY DAY COLLECTION

FACTS IN SUMMARY: CHESTER A. ARTHUR

CHRONOLOGY

UNITED STATES		ARTHUR
	1830	*Born October 5*
Jackson re-elected President	1832	
Van Buren elected President	1836	
Harrison elected President	1840	
Tyler becomes President	1841	
Polk elected President	1844	*Enters Lyceum School in Schenectady*
Annexation of Texas	1845	*Enters Union College as sophomore*
War with Mexico	1846	
Taylor elected President	1848	*Elected to Phi Beta Kappa*
		Graduates from Union College
Fillmore becomes President	1850	
Compromise of 1850		
	1851	*Teaches school in Vermont*
Pierce elected President	1852	*Becomes school principal in Cohoes, N.Y.*
Gadsden Purchase	1853	*Studies law in New York*
		Admitted to the bar
Republican party formed	1854	
Buchanan elected President	1856	
Dred Scott decision	1857	
Lincoln-Douglas debates	1858	
John Brown's raid at Harpers Ferry	1859	*Marries Ellen Lewis Herndon*
Lincoln elected President	1860	
South Carolina secedes		
Fort Sumter fired upon	1861	*Appointed engineer in chief of New York State*
First Battle of Bull Run		
Battle of Shiloh	1862	*Commissioned inspector general of New York troops*
Monitor v. *Merrimac*		*Commissioned quarter-master general of New York State*
Battle of Antietam		
Confederate victory at Fredericksburg		
Emancipation Proclamation	1863	
Battle of Chancellorsville		
Vicksburg Campaign		
Gettysburg Campaign		
Battle of the Wilderness	1864	
Lincoln re-elected President		
Sherman's march to the sea		

UNITED STATES Sept. 19, 1881 — March 4, 1885

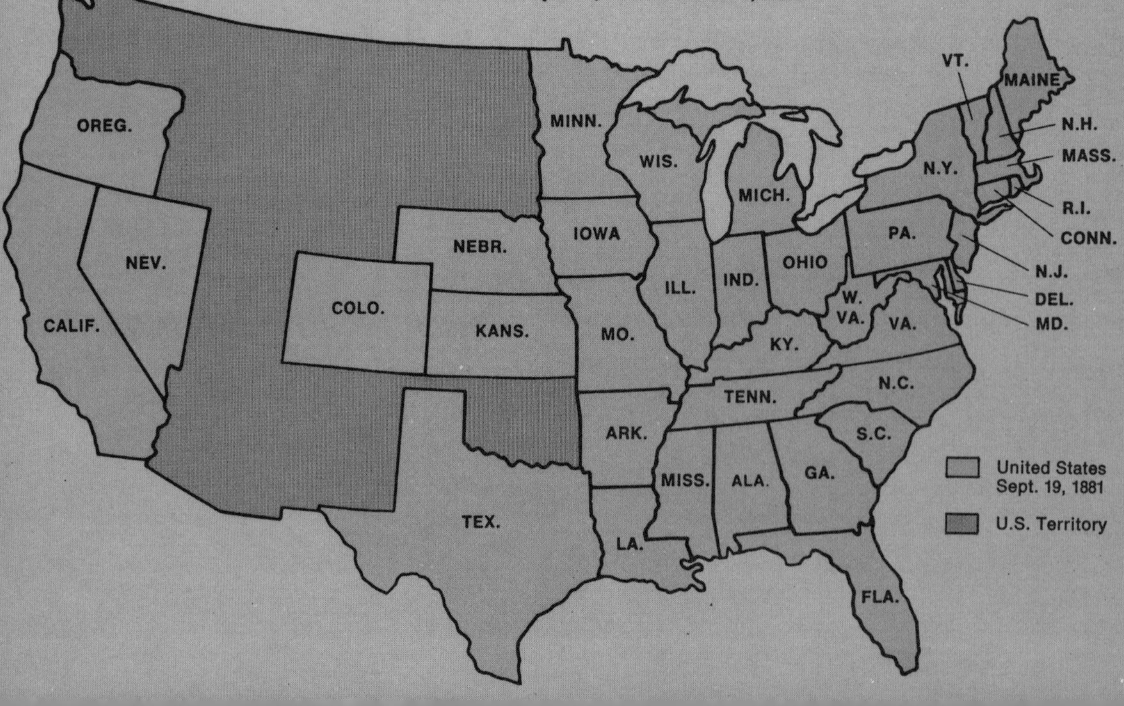

Lee surrenders at Appomattox	1865	
Lincoln assassinated		
Johnson becomes President		
Thirteenth Amendment ratified		
Johnson impeached	1868	
Fourteenth Amendment ratified		
Grant inaugurated as President	1869	*Appointed counsel to the New York City Tax Commission*
	1871	*Named collector of customs for the Port of New York*
Grant re-elected President	1872	
Panic of 1873	1873	
	1875	*Reappointed collector of customs*
Hayes named President after disputed election	1877	
	1878	*Suspended as collector*
Garfield elected President	1880	*Ellen Arthur dies*
		Elected Vice President
Garfield assassinated	1881	*Becomes President*
	1882	*Loses control of Congress*
Pendleton Act	1883	*Signs Pendleton Act*
Cleveland elected President	1884	*Loses presidential nomination to James G. Blaine*
Dedication of the Washington Monument	1885	*Retires to New York City*
	1886	*Dies November 18*

BIOGRAPHICAL FACTS

BIRTH: Fairfield, Vt. (?), Oct. 5, 1830
ANCESTRY: Scotch-Irish and English
FATHER: William Arthur; b. County Antrim, Ireland, 1796; d. Newtonville, N.Y., Oct. 27, 1875
FATHER'S OCCUPATION: Baptist minister
MOTHER: Malvina Stone Arthur; b. Berkshire, Vt., April 24, 1802; d. Newtonville, N.Y., Jan. 16, 1869
BROTHERS: William (1834–1915); George (1836–1838)
SISTERS: Regina (1822–1910); Jane (1824–1842); Almeda (1826–1899); Ann Eliza (1828–1915); Malvina (1832–1920); Mary (1841–1917)
WIFE: Ellen Lewis Herndon; b. Fredericksburg, Va., Aug. 30, 1837; d. New York, N.Y., Jan. 12, 1880
MARRIAGE: New York, N.Y., Oct. 25, 1859
CHILDREN: William Lewis Herndon (1860–1863); Chester Alan, Jr. (1864–1937); Ellen (1871–1915)
EDUCATION: Attended public schools and Lyceum School; graduated with honors from Union College (1848)
RELIGIOUS AFFILIATION: Episcopalian
OCCUPATIONS BEFORE PRESIDENCY: Teacher; school principal; lawyer
PRE-PRESIDENTIAL OFFICES: Quartermaster General of New York State; New York Collector of Customs; Vice President

LIBRARY OF CONGRESS

Virginia-born Ellen Lewis Herndon Arthur, above, died at forty-two, before her husband became President.

POLITICAL PARTY: Republican
AGE AT INAUGURATION: 50
OCCUPATION AFTER PRESIDENCY: Retired
DEATH: New York, N.Y., Nov. 18, 1886
PLACE OF BURIAL: Rural Cemetery, Albany, N.Y.

THE ARTHUR ADMINISTRATION

INAUGURATION: Sept. 20, 1881; New York, N.Y.
SECRETARY OF STATE: James G. Blaine; Frederick T. Frelinghuysen (from Dec. 19, 1881)
SECRETARY OF THE TREASURY: William Windom; Charles J. Folger (from Nov. 14, 1881); Walter Q. Gresham (from Sept. 24, 1884); Hugh McCulloch (from Oct. 31, 1884)
SECRETARY OF WAR: Robert T. Lincoln
ATTORNEY GENERAL: Wayne MacVeagh; Benjamin H. Brewster (from Jan. 3, 1882)
POSTMASTER GENERAL: Thomas L. James; Timothy O. Howe (from Jan. 5, 1882); Walter Q. Gresham (from April 11, 1883); Frank Hatton (from Oct. 14, 1884)
SECRETARY OF THE NAVY: William H. Hunt; William E. Chandler (from April 17, 1882)
SECRETARY OF THE INTERIOR: Samuel J. Kirkwood; Henry M. Teller (from April 17, 1882)
SUPREME COURT APPOINTMENTS: Horace Gray (1881); Samuel Blatchford (1882)
47th CONGRESS (March 4, 1881–March 4, 1883):
Senate: 37 Republicans; 37 Democrats; 1 Other
House: 147 Republicans; 135 Democrats; 11 Others
48th CONGRESS (March 4, 1883–March 4, 1885):
Senate: 38 Republicans; 36 Democrats; 2 Others
House: 197 Democrats; 118 Republicans; 10 Others
END OF PRESIDENTIAL TERM: March 4, 1885

LIBRARY OF CONGRESS

THE TWENTY-SECOND PRESIDENT (1885–1889)
THE TWENTY-FOURTH PRESIDENT (1893–1897)

GROVER CLEVELAND

On March 4, 1885, when Grover Cleveland stood up in the sparkling sun on the east portico of the Capitol to take his presidential oath, he presented an imposing figure. At a burly two hundred and fifty pounds, he was the heftiest Chief Executive the United States had yet had—only the rotund William Howard Taft, at three hundred and forty, would eclipse that record. He was a handsome, beer-drinking, cigar-smoking hunter and fisherman, an indefatigable worker with an inexhaustible store of energy. In a day when government was for sale on the bargain counters of Tammany Hall, when, as Henry Demarest Lloyd put it, "the Standard [Oil Company] has done everything with the Pennsylvania legislature except refine it," Cleveland had the reputation for being "ugly-honest." During his presidential election campaign, when he was attacked over the embarrassing matter of his having sired an illegitimate child, Cleveland gave his aides a directive considered unique in the history of politics: "Tell the truth."

The only Democratic President between 1861 and 1913, Cleveland was also the first and only Chief Executive to serve two nonconsecutive terms. He had entered national politics rather suddenly, as Everyman's hero, a politician of uncompromising independence and integrity. To the surprise and dismay of mentors and opponents alike, he remained incorruptible; by the time he completed his second term, he was despised and had been repudiated by his own party. His stubbornness, in fact, had earned him the title "His Obstinacy."

Born March 18, 1837, in a parsonage in Caldwell, New Jersey, Stephen Grover Cleveland was the fifth of nine children of Ann Neal and Richard Falley Cleveland, the local Presbyterian minister. When the latter secured the job of district secretary for the American Home Mission Society, he moved his family to central New York State, settling eventually in the town of Holland

Grover Cleveland as he appeared in 1892

Patent. From his father the youthful Cleveland learned all of the solid—and some of the stolid—Protestant virtues stressed in provincial America at the time. He memorized the Westminster Confession and *Pilgrim's Progress.* Family worship, as Allan Nevins recorded in his biography of Cleveland, "was held every evening."

The death of his father sent the sixteen-year-old Grover Cleveland out to earn a living. For a while he tried working at a school for the blind in New York City, but at the end of a year he returned to Holland Patent, borrowed twenty-five dollars from an elder of the Presbyterian church, and headed west with another boy from the town. Cleveland got as far as Buffalo; there an uncle, Lewis F. Allen, helped him find a job in a law firm. Seldom venturing far until he was elected governor, he spent the next twenty-six years in Buffalo, a growing brawny town of iron foundries, breweries, furniture factories, and docks busy with Great Lakes traffic.

Sometimes laboring through the night without sleep, Grover Cleveland worked doggedly at learning the law. After he was admitted to the bar in 1859, he worked just as hard, and by the middle of the 1870's he was a moderately well-to-do Buffalo lawyer. A stubborn man, he guarded his independence fiercely and was given to irritability and even wrathfulness when he felt it threatened. Equally fierce was his determination, and his corporation clientele found it more than worthwhile to tolerate his independence. Cleveland avoided ties that might make his time less than his own, remaining unmarried and refusing, for example, a lucrative job with the New York Central Railroad because he did not want to travel when it might be inconvenient. For many years he spent his leisure time in boisterous male company at the better local saloons, but in 1877 he helped found the City Club and took to wearing very correct clothes and a top hat.

From outward appearances Cleveland was a dull, unimaginative, even passionless man—a plodder. Yet, outward appearances do not tell the whole story. Cautious, preserving a proper façade, Cleveland charted a course of political advancement for himself. If his comrades did not believe him an ambitious man, it was only because they could not comprehend a man who wished to pursue political goals without the customary wheeling and dealing.

BUFFALO AND ERIE COUNTY HISTORICAL SOCIETY

Cleveland was a promising young Buffalo, New York, lawyer when this photograph was taken about 1864.

As early as 1858, Cleveland had worked for the local Democratic organization as a volunteer helping to get out the vote. In 1862 he was a delegate to the city convention. That same year, at the age of twenty-five, he was elected a ward supervisor; he was soon after appointed assistant district attorney. He served in this capacity for three years, learning a good deal about crime and corruption, and through his experiences he undoubtedly arrived at conclusions about how government ought to be run. As Nevins put it, "He was completely lacking in martial spirit" and so avoided fighting in the Civil War by furnishing a substitute—not at all an uncommon procedure at the time.

In 1865 Cleveland ran for district attorney, lost, and spent the next few years building up his law practice. In 1870 he ran for sheriff of Erie County—an office that no other reputable, or disreputable, lawyer would have considered worth the trouble—and won by a mere 303 votes. After serving as sheriff for three years, Cleveland joined Lyman K. Bass and Wilson S. Bissell in a law firm that soon became one of the most prominent in Buffalo. Cleveland himself rarely appeared in court, took modest fees and very brief vacations, and saved his money. He gained considerable weight drinking beer and eating sausages at Schenkelberger's Restaurant, played pinochle and poker, owned one of the best bird dogs in town, and had at least one fist fight—with a Mike Falvey, over Democratic politics. Then, in 1881, as Horace Samuel Merrill wrote, "Public indignation placed Grover Cleveland on the road to fame."

If the 1880's were years of "robber barons" and burgeoning trusts, of railroad empires and fights for the regulation of railroads, of rampant discontent among farmers, of industrial warfare and the birth of unions, they were at least in equal measure years of the dirtiest government America had ever seen. It was a time when politicians were bought and sold a dozen times over. *Harper's Weekly* proclaimed the United States Senate "a club of rich men . . . not sensitive to the charge of voting upon questions in which they have a pecuniary interest," a Senate corrupt and indifferent to public opinion.

But there were, of course, reformers, and in 1881 a Buffalo reform group decided to try for city hall. They approached a number of honest men with political experience, but none wanted the thankless job of mayor of Buffalo. So Grover Cleveland became their candidate. He campaigned hard for the office and won without spending a penny for drinks-all-around in the saloons and without making a single political deal.

Within a year of taking office, Cleveland saved Buffalo one million dollars simply by vetoing fraudulent sewage and street-cleaning contracts. He was given to pointing out, with indignant anger, those portions of bills that were nakedly graft grabbing. Crookedness was genuinely offensive to him. Surprisingly enough, he was equally candid about his own mistakes, reversing one of his decisions with the statement: "I desire to acknowledge that my action in the matter was hasty and inconsiderate. A little examination and reflection would have prevented it." It was remarkably impolitic of him—with the result that the Buffalo *Sunday Times* editorially proposed that he would make an excellent governor.

Cleveland did not solicit partisans in his bid for the governorship—in fact, he positively avoided any political alliances—but support flocked to him. He was nominated to oppose Republican Charles J. Folger, a good man who had the bad luck to appear a mere puppet of Chester A. Arthur and the ever-popular villain, Jay Gould. Cleveland captured thousands of Republican votes. Having incurred no political debts of significance, he was elected, as biographer Robert McElroy wrote, as the "unowned candidate."

Early in Cleveland's term as governor, the legislature passed a bill intended to reduce the fare on the rich, Jay Gould-controlled New York City elevated railway to five cents at all times. The "el" could well afford a nickel fare, but charged ten cents during off-hours. The bill was designed to be a slap on the wrist to Gould. Cleveland, who was no friend of Gould's, nevertheless vetoed the bill, pointing out that to reduce the fare

NEW YORK PUBLIC LIBRARY

The Puck *cartoon at right shows the de-clawed Tammany tiger "made harmless at last" by Cleveland and his young ally, Assemblyman Teddy Roosevelt.*

without a careful examination of the company's finances was a violation of the right of contract protected by the First Amendment. His veto message, though unexpected and eminently impolitic, was so logical, so legally and morally correct, that he received surprisingly little criticism.

Cleveland managed, too—by thwarting Tammany moves to appoint incompetents to public office—to utterly alienate John Kelly of Tammany Hall. Kelly was a dangerous enemy. Without New York State, a presidential candidate stood little chance, and without Tammany, it was generally agreed, New York could not be carried. Yet it was Cleveland's stubborn opposition to Tammany that captured the imagination of the voters and made him a national figure.

In June of 1884 the Republicans convened in Chicago to nominate their candidate for President. A small but distinguished group of reformers—soon known as Mugwumps—was present, headed by Carl Schurz, New York legislator Theodore Roosevelt, President Charles Eliot of Harvard, Henry Ward Beecher, Charles Francis Adams, Jr., Leverett Saltonstall, and Henry Cabot Lodge. The machine Republicans treated them with contempt—noting that they "had their hair parted in the middle" and were "neither male nor female" but some aberration. The convention nominated James G. Blaine, who as Speaker of the House had allegedly sold railroad stocks and bonds under the shadiest of circumstances. The reformers bolted their party, and the Democrats, meeting in Chicago in July, responded by nominating Cleveland on the second ballot.

There followed one of the most memorable mud-slinging campaigns in American politics. Blaine's correspondence with the Boston firm that had handled his stock transactions was published in a local newspaper by the Mugwumps. On the back of one note, written in 1876, Blaine had scrawled, "Burn this letter!" And so the Democrats had their campaign song:

Blaine, Blaine, James G. Blaine,
The continental liar from the State of Maine,
Burn this letter!

In Cleveland's past, the Republicans discovered a Mrs. Maria Halpin, who claimed that the candidate was the father of her illegitimate son. It was not certain who the boy's father was, but Cleveland could have been, and he accepted the responsibility. It was on this occasion that Cleveland made his famous reply to a friend who asked how to respond to the charge: "Tell the truth." The Republicans then sang:

Ma! Ma! Where's my pa?
Gone to the White House.
Ha! Ha! Ha!

But the balance swung against Blaine. A Chicagoan suggested: "We are told that Mr. Blaine has been delinquent in office but blameless in private life, while Mr. Cleveland has been a model of official integrity, but culpable in his personal relations. We should therefore elect Mr. Cleveland to the public office which he is so well qualified to fill, and remand Mr. Blaine to the private station which he is admirably fitted to adorn." And most of the country adopted that position. The Mugwumps drew to Cleveland's support most, if not all, the reformists of the country; Beecher and Schurz led the contingent from New York. Nearly the entire Eastern press fell behind Cleveland.

Blaine made two crucial blunders. He was present at a speech by the Reverend Dr. Samuel Burchard in New York. Burchard said: "We are Republicans and don't propose to leave our party and identify ourselves with the party whose antecedents have been *rum, Romanism and rebellion*." Blaine, no doubt tired from campaigning, missed the obvious slur against the Catholics and did not dissociate himself from it. Overnight he lost the loyalty of 500,000 Irish voters in the all-important state of New York, not to mention the Catholics in the rest of the nation. On the very same day —six days before the election—he was present at a dinner in his honor, offered by Jay Gould and Russell Sage, at Delmonico's in New York. The next day Joseph Pulitzer's newspaper, the New York *World*, reported in banner headlines: "THE ROYAL FEAST OF

J. DOYLE DEWITT COLLECTION

Campaign gadgets, such as this splendid Cleveland noisemaker, were loud in support of their candidate.

BELSHAZZAR BLAINE AND THE MONEY KINGS . . . AN OCCASION FOR THE COLLECTION OF A REPUBLICAN CORRUPTION FUND."

Blaine was finished. Politicians had been deserting him all along. Boss Roscoe Conkling, asked why he had not campaigned for Blaine, had said: "I do not engage in criminal practice." The voters turned to Cleveland, who won the election with a plurality of almost 30,000 votes.

The campaign had hardly dealt with issues, but Cleveland knew precisely what he wanted done. At first he did not consider his role that of a leader of Congress, but believed his job to be one of executing laws and administering the business of the Executive. He waited, therefore, until Congress presented him with problems. In the meantime, he unearthed abuses that came under his jurisdiction. He recovered from the railroads thousands of acres of land that they had held under an exaggeratedly broad interpretation of their land grants and opened them to homesteaders. He reversed a decision of President Arthur's opening up 494,778 acres of Indian land to settlers and land speculators and returned the land to the Indian reservation. He vetoed a bill calling for payments to all Civil War veterans who could claim *any* disability—including old age. He began to reform the civil service. He took great pains to assure that his appointees to the new Interstate Commerce Commission (created by the precedent-breaking Interstate Commerce Act of 1887) would be fair-minded, effective men. But his first three years in office were spent primarily in battling with the endless stream of office seekers who bedeviled him, cajoled him, pressured him—and angered him. "The d——d everlasting clatter for offices continues . . ." Cleveland wrote to a friend, "and makes me feel like resigning and hell is to pay generally." He was threatened with blackmail by at least one New York politician. Joseph Pulitzer's *World* accused him of ingratitude to the loyal workers who put him in office. When Cleveland relented somewhat, Carl Schurz wrote him: "Your attempt to please both reformers and spoilsmen has failed. I warned you more than once that your principal danger was to sit down between two chairs." Schurz should have known better; no one ever warned Cleveland. Cleveland broke off his alliance with Schurz and the Mugwumps.

Even Cleveland's civil service record was, according to the usually sympathetic Nevins, "fumbling and uneven." The President finally replaced 80,000 of 120,000 federal bureaucrats during his first term. Nonetheless, by the end of his second term, he managed to double the number of jobs not subject to patronage. For all the limitedness of the change, it was significant—and it was to alter the very nature of party control. It sharply curtailed the leverage the President was able to use to gain congressional support by promising jobs for votes. For Cleveland personally, it crystallized the hostility of Tammany Hall (one of the factors that cost him the Presidency in 1888), and it set the tone of wrangling with congressmen that was to prevail throughout his career.

Until his election to the Presidency, Cleveland's political record presented a one-dimensional picture of an honest man fighting corruption with little initiative or bold leadership. The character of his career changed, interestingly enough, just after he was married, on June 2, 1886, to the pretty, dark-eyed, twenty-one-year-old Frances Folsom, daughter of one of his Buffalo law partners. He had considered himself her virtual guardian from the time her father died in 1875 and had entertained her and her mother at the White House for ten days in 1885. He proposed to her shortly after her graduation from Wells College. They were married in the White House to the strains of the wedding march played by John Phillip Sousa. Mrs. Cleveland brightened Washington society and her husband's life. He became far more sociable, took more vacations, was generally less irritable, and displayed a more positive, bold leadership with legislators.

As Congress opened its session in the autumn of 1886, Cleveland moved immediately on the two most prominent issues of the eighties other than civil service reform: preservation of the gold standard and the lowering of the tariff. He made little headway in trying to prevent the coinage of silver (the real battle lay ahead, with William Jennings Bryan, in Cleveland's second term). But he mustered all his strength on the tariff question, and in December of 1887, he broke all precedents and devoted his entire annual message to Congress to it. He attacked all tariffs on necessities—those tariffs which were an undoubted hardship on farmers and laborers. He declined to compromise in any way with the powerful business interests that mobilized against him.

Some reduction in the tariff had been recognized as essential. A growing Treasury surplus was keeping excessive amounts of money out of circulation, and most politicians proposed a reduction in internal revenue taxation. Cleveland attacked head on. He observed that on the one hand Americans were boasting with a series of centennial celebrations of the strength and accomplishment of American industry and that on the other hand—when the tariff question was raised—"it suits the purposes of advocacy to call our manufacturers infant industries still needing the highest and greatest degree of favor and fostering care that can be wrung from Federal legislation." He castigated trusts and called the tariff laws "vicious."

Before his tariff message, Cleveland had been considered a shoo-in for re-election. But he had said to a friend: "What is the use of being elected or re-elected unless you stand for something?" He was through playing safe. The House passed a tariff measure of which Cleveland could approve with some reservation. Before the Senate could act, however, the election campaign was in full swing and the issue of the tariff was obscured by the tumult.

Although the voters endorsed him with a plurality of nearly 100,000 votes, Cleveland lost to Republican Benjamin Harrison by 223 electoral votes to 168. Tammany Hall, in an alliance with the Republicans, took New York from him; the tariff cost him several other key states. Cleveland left office having accomplished little indeed. His first term was important principally in that he acquired a more certain sense of leadership.

In his last annual message to Congress, Cleveland decried cities where "wealth and luxury" existed callously beside "poverty and wretchedness and unremunerative toil." "The gulf between employers and the employed," he said, "is constantly widening, and classes are rapidly forming. . . ." Corporations, he warned, were "fast becoming the people's masters" while the farmers were struggling against "impoverishment." Perhaps his greatest limitation was that he believed that lowering the tariff would solve most of these difficulties.

Out of office, Cleveland watched with growing uneasiness as the "Billion-Dollar Congress" handed out liberal Civil War pensions, passed the high McKinley Tariff, and placed a severe strain on the gold standard by passing the Sherman Silver-Purchase Act. But he enjoyed private life and spent some of the most pleasurable weeks of his life vacationing and fishing at Buzzards Bay on Cape Cod. He wrote to a friend that "the inclination is growing on me, daily, to permit things other than politics to claim the greatest share of my attention."

Cleveland's most important public act during his four years out of office was to write his famous "silver letter" in 1891, in which he condemned "the dangerous and reckless experiment of free, unlimited, and independent silver coinage." Once again, all the Democrats were horrified by what they considered an impolitic maneuver, and it is not clear, in judging this one action of Cleveland's, whether or not he was for once trying to throw away his political career—so completely had he taken to private life. Nonetheless, in the following year he was nominated by the Democrats on the first ballot, and in the election he routed Harrison, winning a plurality of 400,000 popular votes.

Cleveland took office in his second term at a time when the country was far more restless than it had been in several decades. The Populist candidate for President had won more than a million votes in the 1892 election. William Jennings Bryan had been elected to Congress a year earlier. Eugene V. Debs had just organized the American Railway Union, which, by 1893, had 150,000 members. The General Managers' Association—which employed 221,000 workers—formed to combat the unions. Beneath the glitter of the new skyscrapers and electric lights, a class war was brewing in America. Ten days before Cleveland took office, the Philadelphia and Reading Railroad, with debts of over $125,000,000, went bankrupt. Immediately after his inauguration the great National Cordage Company collapsed, setting off a panic on Wall Street. The Atchison, Topeka and Santa Fe was exposed for defrauding the public of $7,000,000. The Treasury gold reserve dropped below the $100,000,000 mark—considered the balance necessary to guarantee solid money. Some five hundred banks failed before the end of

LIBRARY OF CONGRESS

THOMAS A. HENDRICKS

Thomas A. Hendricks, Cleveland's running mate in 1884, was Indiana's favorite son, an old guard Democrat, and the "soft-money" candidate of the West. Raised on a farm in Shelby County, Indiana, Hendricks took up the study of law, was admitted to the bar, and became a successful attorney. In 1848 the twenty-nine-year-old Hoosier entered the state legislature and later served as a delegate to the state constitutional convention. In 1851 he became a United States representative and in 1855 was appointed commissioner of the General Land Office. Elected to the Senate in 1863, he served for one term as an outspoken critic of the Republican administration. Attacking the draft and heavy taxation, he also opposed general emancipation on the grounds that it was a local matter and that the Negro was indeed inferior. Rising to prominence in the Democratic party, he was a contender for the presidential nomination in 1868, and in 1872 he was elected governor of Indiana. Four years later he became the Democratic candidate for Vice President and was narrowly defeated with Samuel J. Tilden in the contested election. When reformer Grover Cleveland was nominated for the Presidency in 1884, Hendricks was chosen for the second spot to appease the party machine and to strengthen the ticket in the Middle West. His term as Vice President was cut short when he died in November, 1885.

ADLAI E. STEVENSON

Less prominent than his famous namesake grandson, Adlai Ewing Stevenson nonetheless attained a higher office. Elected to the Vice Presidency in 1892, he served under Cleveland for four years as second in command. A country lawyer from Illinois, Stevenson was almost forty when he won a Democratic seat in the House of Representatives in 1874. During two nonconsecutive terms in Congress, he represented the soft-money, low-tariff views of the Midwestern farmer and laborer. As first assistant postmaster general during Cleveland's first term, it was his unpleasant task to remove some forty thousand Republican postmasters to provide jobs for Democratic supporters. Not surprisingly, his subsequent nomination as supreme court justice of the District of Columbia was rejected by a hostile Republican majority in the Senate. When Cleveland, a "hard-money" man, was renominated by the Democrats in 1892, Stevenson was placed on the ticket to please the inflationist forces. Presiding over the Senate with tact and diplomacy, he remained loyal to the administration in spite of his opposite economic views. In 1900 Stevenson ran for Vice President on the Democratic ticket headed by William Jennings Bryan. Eight years later he was narrowly defeated for the governorship of Illinois. Retiring from public life, Stevenson published his memoirs in 1909 and died at the age of eighty in June, 1914.

1893. Mortgages were foreclosed. Within a year, an estimated two to three million American workers were unemployed.

Cleveland's response to the financial panic was to call for the repeal of the Sherman Silver-Purchase Act in an attempt to restore confidence in the American dollar. Westerners and Southerners clamored for silver coinage, believing that if more money were put in circulation the plight of the farmers and laborers would be alleviated. Cleveland firmly believed in Gresham's Law (that bad money drives out good) and insisted on maintaining the gold standard.

As Chief Executive, this was Cleveland's finest hour. He called for a special session of Congress to repeal the Sherman act. Then, in the very midst of preparation for the battle, Cleveland noticed a rough spot on the roof of his mouth. His doctor advised immediate removal of the cancerous growth, and in order to avoid plunging the country into further panic, Cleveland boarded a yacht in New York and sailed to Buzzards Bay, having the whole of his upper left jaw removed on the way. He debarked at Buzzards Bay and set to work immediately on his message for the special session. (The operation left its mark; Cleveland, though still strong, never again was able to work the long hours he had for so many years. He tired easily, and irritability burst to the surface more frequently.)

Cleveland's leadership of Congress was strong and purposeful. Daniel W. Voorhees of Indiana, the chairman of the powerful Senate Finance Committee, had opposed Cleveland's renomination in 1892 and had been a champion of silver coinage for two decades. His arguments in the Senate would be crucial. He utterly surprised his colleagues by leading the fight for repeal on Cleveland's behalf. The reason for the dramatic switch emerges from Cleveland's correspondence: he had promised all Indiana patronage to Voorhees.

After two months of fights, filibusters, and the sight of grown men reduced to tears in the Senate, the legislators came up with a compromise plan and presented it to Cleveland. The President reportedly erupted in anger, banged his fist on a table, and announced that he would not yield. A moderate statement was issued to the press: "The President adheres to the position that the purchasing clause of the Sherman silver law should be unconditionally repealed. . . ." His refusal to admit defeat heartened his followers, and ten days later, on October 30, 1893, the Sherman Silver-Purchase Act was repealed.

After repeal, Secretary of the Treasury John Carlisle, in an effort to shore up the federal gold reserve, twice issued $50,000,000 worth of bonds in 1894. When the public did not respond to the offering, he was compelled to issue the bonds to Wall Street bankers, who simply cashed in their old notes at the New York Sub-Treasury to obtain the gold to buy the new bonds. Nothing was gained; by January, 1895, the Treasury was losing gold at a rate of $3,000,000 a day. Then J. P. Morgan offered to raise $50,000,000 in gold for the government—half of it to come from abroad—and to ensure that it would not be immediately withdrawn. At 3.75 per cent the interest rate was high, but the main provision was that the government not make a public bond issue again and deal with Morgan alone.

The terms seemed too stiff to Cleveland, and he made preparations for another public issue. A bill was introduced in Congress, where it was defeated on February 7, 1895. At the very moment when Congress was voting, Morgan was on the train from New York. He was greeted in Washington by one of Cleveland's aides and told that the President could not see him that evening. Furious, Morgan said he would get back on the train and let the country go bankrupt. He was persuaded to stay, however, and sat up all night in his hotel room playing solitaire.

The next morning Morgan and Cleveland met at the White House; neither would yield. Then the phone rang; a Treasury official informed the President that there was less than $9,000,000 in gold at the New York Sub-Treasury. Morgan knew of an outstanding note for $12,000,000. "Mr. President," he said, ". . . if that [note] is presented today; it is all over." The stubborn, independent Cleveland, the man who responded to coercion with contrariness, gave in.

That Cleveland did acquiesce indicated just how critical the situation was. To most of the country it indicated something far more frightening as well: the unrestricted power of J. P. Morgan. Imprecations fell upon Cleveland with a vengeance. The silverites rose up to condemn him, and Cleveland, in saving the gold standard, had lost the Democratic party to the Populists.

Cleveland, however, had two significant foreign policy achievements in his second term. During Harrison's tenure a treaty to annex Hawaii had been negotiated and sent to the Senate for ratification. Five days after taking office, Cleveland recalled the treaty and quashed it. Some Hawaiians, to be sure, wanted to join America. Most, however, did not. "If national honesty is to be disregarded," Cleveland said in a message to Congress, "and a desire for territorial expansion or dissatisfaction with a form of government not our own ought to regulate our conduct, I have entirely misapprehended the . . . character of our government. . . ."

A drawn-out dispute with Great Britain, dating from 1887, finally exhausted Cleveland's patience in 1895. The crux of the disagreement was over the boundary between British Guiana and Venezuela. Cleveland, invoking the ever-handy Monroe Doctrine, maintained that Britain was attempting to expand its interests in the Americas. He has been criticized for the vehemence with which he finally attacked Great Britain over the matter. Yet, however bellicose his words, he labored to stem any jingoism that might have followed his message, and he brought the issue to arbitration quickly. As Nevins has noted, Cleveland's move had an important side effect in "clearing the atmosphere between Great Britain and the United States" and initiating "a virtual *entente* that within a generation was to prove of the profoundest importance in world history."

Despite such accomplishments, the conflicting forces of the nineties ultimately overwhelmed Cleveland. His fight for a reduction in the tariff, swamped by the strong economic interests that effectively controlled Congress, resulted in the passage of the Wilson-Gorman Tariff, which maintained high tariffs.

The period from July of 1894 to July of 1895, Nevins wrote, "might well be called the *année terrible* of American history between Reconstruction and the World War." It was the year in which Morgan engineered his loan to the government, the year of the Chicago Pullman strike and Coxey's march on Washington, a year in which 750,000 laborers went out on strikes. Cleveland, wrangling with Congress, striking out bitterly at legislators after the passage of the tariff, earned in that year the title "His Obstinacy," and he made repeated mistakes in the handling of labor disputes.

Cleveland's first mistake had been the selection of the hot-tempered, pugnacious Richard Olney of Massachusetts as his Attorney General. Olney—with Cleveland's endorsement, to be sure—applied inexcusably harsh measures in putting down the unemployed citizens, led by Populist Jacob S. Coxey, who marched on Washington to petition for relief. "Coxey's Army" had originally contained more than 25,000 protesters from various parts of the nation, but only about 400 actually reached the Capitol; they were dispersed by police, and many were beaten.

Later in 1894, Cleveland and Olney permitted themselves to be panicked once again when workmen of the Pullman Palace Car Company in Chicago, locked out of their jobs after striking against a wage reduction and the injustices of company-owned stores and homes, allied themselves with Eugene V. Debs's American Railway Union. By the end of the month, a boycott of Pullman cars on all Midwestern railroads had been established, and after Olney swore in 3,400 special deputies, violence erupted. Then Olney (who had been one of the founders of the General Managers' Association, which was backing Pullman) overrode the objections of Illinois's courageous governor, John Altgeld, and—with Cleveland's approval—sent federal troops to restore order in Chicago. The strike was broken by an injunction, and Debs was sent to jail, where he first read the writings of Karl Marx.

The famous Pullman strike, and its aftermath, pointed up Grover Cleveland's most serious limitation as President. Although Cleveland had foreseen the increasing discontent among American workers and had spoken of it in his message to Congress in 1887, although he was the first President to address a message to Congress concerning labor (calling for a permanent labor-management mediation panel in 1886), he had never really acquainted himself with laborers and their problems. It was in fact a parochialism of the middle class that limited his vision and motivated many of his intemperate and sometimes frightened reactions to both the rich and the poor.

On December 3, 1895, Cleveland delivered his annual State of the Union message to Congress. Only four persons applauded it. The silverites, headed by William Jennings Bryan, had the loyalty of the Democrats. When the Democrats met in 1896, "Pitchfork" Ben Tillman addressed the convention: "We denounce the Administration of President Cleveland as undemocratic and tyrannical. . . ." William Jennings Bryan, his moment having come, made his famous "Cross of Gold" speech and was nominated; in the election that followed, Cleveland was all but forgotten.

Cleveland's reputation did not revive until many years after he left office. But, by the time he died on June 24, 1908, he was a much-respected elder statesman—admired for the stand he took in the Venezuelan border dispute, for the principles he enunciated in the controversy over Hawaii, for his defiance of machine politics, for his dauntless fight for the gold standard. He has finally been accounted a "near-great" President, and he does remain the archetype of a President who stood against political expediency, a man who, right or wrong, said, "Tell the truth."

—CHARLES L. MEE, JR.

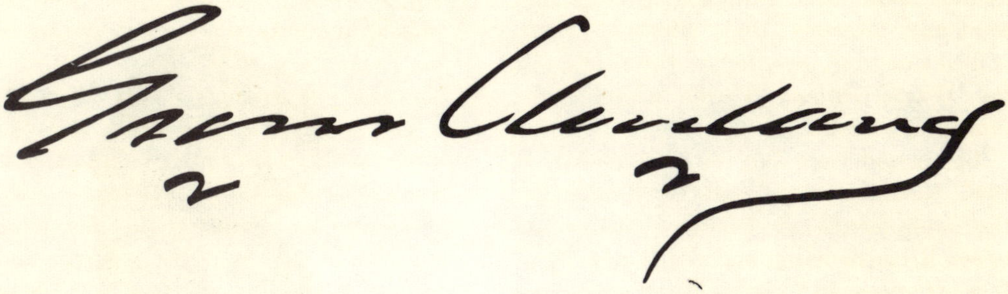

A PICTURE PORTFOLIO

J. DOYLE DEWITT COLLECTION

Grover Cleveland's stern visage adorns the Democratic campaign medal above.

LIBRARY OF CONGRESS

JAMES G. BLAINE

In James G. Blaine, the magnetic and eloquent "Plumed Knight" of the Republican party, Grover Cleveland had a formidable opponent for the Presidency. Born in Pennsylvania in 1830, Blaine settled in Augusta, Maine, entered the state legislature, and became the acknowledged leader of the Maine Republicans. Elected to Congress in 1862, he served for almost two decades as representative, Speaker of the House, and senator. As leader of the liberal element of the party, Blaine was an attractive presidential prospect. But charges of graft in his dealings with the railroads cost him the nomination in 1876, and he was thwarted again in 1880. In 1884 he finally became the Republican candidate; but the railroad scandal continued to hurt him, and a supporter's reference to the opposition as the party of "rum, Romanism, and rebellion" alienated the Irish Catholics in the key state of New York. Defeated by Cleveland, Blaine returned to foreign affairs. In 1881 he had been Secretary of State under Garfield. Supporting Harrison in 1888, he again became Secretary and resumed his fight for a more constructive Latin-American policy. A statesman of vision, he was instrumental in organizing the first Pan-American Conference, in formulating policy for a United States-controlled Isthmian canal, and in increasing trade with Latin America. Blaine died in Washington in January, 1893.

BOTH: J. DOYLE DEWITT COLLECTION

The penny-bank figure (top) shows the Greenback candidate, Benjamin Butler, in the unflattering form of a frog. A Civil War general and a former governor of Massachusetts, Butler ran on both the Greenback and Anti-Monopoly tickets in 1884.

Mrs. Belva Lockwood, candidate of the National Equal Rights party in 1884 and 1888, was the first woman to run for President. A prominent Washington lawyer (the first woman to plead before the Supreme Court), she often rode through the Capital on her three-wheeled cycle, snug in her red stockings.

REFORM CANDIDATE

"Fire and smoke burst from the nostrils of Tammany," reported the New York *Sun* when the Brooklyn delegation to the 1884 Democratic convention declared its votes for Cleveland. The former mayor of Buffalo and governor of New York, Grover Cleveland, had alienated New York's powerful Tammany Hall bosses with his reforms, and they were out to block his nomination at all costs. "Cleveland cannot carry the State of New York," proclaimed Tammany henchman Thomas Grady. Tired of Tammany's greed and interference, Edward Bragg of Wisconsin spoke for those who favored the reform candidate. "They love Cleveland for his character," he said, "but they love him also for the enemies he has made." Furiously, Tammany boss John Kelly shouted in response, "In behalf of his enemies, I accept your statement." When the uproar subsided, Cleveland led the first ballot by 224 votes. A last-ditch effort by the marplots to effect a coalition failed, and Cleveland was nominated on the second ballot. The ensuing campaign was a low-level affair. Republicans spread the story of Cleveland's illegitimate son, and Democrats dug up an old railroad scandal involving the Republican candidate, James G. Blaine. But despite the muckraking, a feeling prevailed that Cleveland would restore "good government"; that his election would prove, as one hopeful put it, that "in the end . . . there *is* a public conscience. . . ."

The cartoon above, which appeared in the Republican weekly Judge, *was captioned "Another Voice for Cleveland." Having acknowledged an illegitimate son, "Grover the Good" is plagued by an embarrassing squall.*

Frances Folsom Cleveland (photographed above in her ivory-satin wedding dress) was only twenty-one when she married the forty-nine-year-old bachelor President in 1886. A "tall, very pretty and direct person," she was "the most popular of First Ladies" and made things lively at the White House.

A NEW FIRST LADY

"The White House under its young mistress will now be the scene of charming festivities," predicted *Harper's Weekly* after Cleveland's marriage to the lovely Frances Folsom on June 2, 1886. The ceremony—attended only by the Cabinet, a few close friends, and members of the families—"called a momentary truce to partisan hostility" and generated great public interest. No incident relating to the union was too trivial to be newsworthy, and the couple was beleaguered by an overzealous press. Not even on their honeymoon were they accorded privacy. Reporters followed them to their Maryland retreat, camped near their cottage, and spied on them with field glasses. Enraged by such "colossal impertinence," the President issued a public statement condemning the "professional gossips" for "doing their utmost to make American journalism contemptible. . . ." On another occasion, when reporters continued to hound his wife, he interrupted a speech, and with tears of indignation, rebuked "those ghouls" who would "desecrate every sacred relation of private life."

But if the public hungered for gossip of the First Lady it was out of love, not malice; and Washington was delighted with its new hostess. Standing at a White House reception—a grace of violets at her waist—she would sometimes receive as many as eight thousand callers and had a warm smile of welcome for each. Lively, bright, and unaffected, she softened the edges of her husband's abrasive personality and won the admiration even of his political enemies. The remark of one who managed to resist the First Lady's charms is perhaps the greatest tribute to her universal appeal: "I detest him so much," exclaimed one of President Cleveland's detractors, "that I don't even think his wife is beautiful."

CHICAGO HISTORICAL SOCIETY

A drawing of Frances Cleveland as the queen of hearts (left) adorned the cover of Judge *magazine in October of 1887. The winsome First Lady is portrayed as the President's greatest drawing card, with the caustic commentary: "What a pity it is for Grover that Hearts are not Trumps in politics."*

The wedding of President Cleveland and his former ward, Frances Folsom (below), was an unprecedented event in the White House. The bride's fifteen-foot train was a sensation with society writers, but as one observer noted, "It was the woman at whom the women looked rather than the dress."

CULVER PICTURES

CAPTAINS OF INDUSTRY

LIBRARY OF CONGRESS

ANDREW CARNEGIE

With a perceptive eye toward the future, Andrew Carnegie saw in the emerging steel industry of the 1870's the road to America's industrial supremacy and to the accumulation of his fortune. Carnegie came to the United States with his impoverished Scotch parents in 1848 at the age of thirteen and began work in a Pennsylvania factory at $1.20 a week. The next year he became a telegraph messenger, was later promoted to operator, and in 1853 was hired by the Pennsylvania Railroad, where he became superintendent of the Pittsburgh Division. In 1865 he formed the highly successful Keystone Bridge Company, and by 1873 he had amassed a considerable fortune. Gambling all his money on the future of American steel, he started his own mills and applied his organizational genius to the development of the industry. Within three decades the Carnegie Company led the nation in steel production. Selling out to U.S. Steel in 1901, Carnegie retired to distribute his fortune "for the improvement of mankind," in keeping with his famous article, "The Gospel of Wealth." Among his endowments were those to public libraries and for the furtherance of education, scientific research, and world peace. Before his death in 1919 Carnegie organized various corporations to continue distribution of his wealth.

BROWN BROTHERS

JOHN D. ROCKEFELLER

John D. Rockefeller's spectacular rise in the oil industry began in 1859 with the drilling of the first well in Titusville, Pennsylvania. Foreseeing an almost limitless market for the "black gold," Rockefeller—still in his early twenties—dissolved a successful wholesaling partnership to establish a Cleveland oil refinery in 1863. Two years later he joined with his brother William to found the Standard Oil Works, and within five years he was president of a corporation that controlled about one-tenth of the nation's refining industry. Buying up pipelines, railroad facilities, and rival companies, Rockefeller proceeded to absorb or eliminate his major competition until, in 1881, Standard Oil was organized into a trust that monopolized the industry. Running counter to the spirit of free enterprise, the monopoly incurred public hostility that mounted until antitrust action dissolved the combination into a number of separate companies in 1911. Having relinquished all but nominal control of the organization by 1897, Rockefeller devoted his remaining forty years to philanthropic pursuits. In 1889 he founded the University of Chicago. Later, with a fortune of nearly a billion dollars, he set up four major institutions to dispense a large portion of his wealth for various worthy purposes. He was ninety-seven when he died in 1937.

LIBRARY OF CONGRESS

JOHN PIERPONT MORGAN

Monarch of a vast financial empire, John Pierpont Morgan began his career in 1856, when he entered his father's banking business. Fifteen years later, he established his own New York firm and built the colossal house of J. P. Morgan & Company. Like the great industrialists of his day, Morgan rose to power through consolidation and centralization of control. During the 1880's and 1890's his reorganization of America's railroads concentrated enormous financial power in the hands of his firm. A prominent government financier, he was called upon by the Cleveland administration to relieve the Treasury crisis of 1895 (which he did at a huge profit to himself), and in the Panic of 1907 his leadership again rescued the economy. Financing such giant corporations as United States Steel in 1901 and International Harvester in 1902, his power became frightening to the American public. A congressional investigation of 1912, however, failed to prove his involvement in an alleged money trust, and he died the next year with his prestige intact. As a critic wrote sometime later, "The Morgan sins, if any, were the sins of magnificence." No less magnificent were Morgan's superb collections of art and literary treasures, now housed in the Metropolitan Museum of Art and the Pierpont Morgan Library in New York City.

CULVER PICTURES

JAY COOKE

Jay Cooke was one of the nation's most influential and public-spirited bankers during the Civil War and the years preceding the Panic of 1873. Born in the Western Reserve (at what is now Sandusky, Ohio), Cooke began clerking in a local store when he was fourteen. Moving to Philadelphia, he became a canal packet clerk and then began in the banking business in 1839. By 1861 he had his own prosperous firm of Jay Cooke & Company. During the Civil War, when government funds were insufficient to meet growing military demands, Cooke established a Washington, D.C., office and came to the nation's rescue. Acting as fiscal agent of the United States Treasury, he secured some two and a half million dollars in loans for the government at a negligible profit to himself. After the war he turned his attentions to the railroads that were pushing west across the continent and was persuaded to finance a northern route to the Pacific. Before the Northern Pacific Railroad could be completed, however, the Cooke company was forced into bankruptcy. Cooke's failure precipitated the Panic of 1873 and left his competitor, John Pierpont Morgan, dominant in American finance. During the next thirty-two years Jay Cooke not only recovered his losses, but was able to repay his creditors completely.

CHICAGO HISTORICAL SOCIETY

The first Democratic victory in twenty-four years was lampooned by Judge *magazine in the 1884 cartoon above, entitled "Democracy's Debut." Emblazoned with such mottoes as "Reform" and "Free trade," the ungainly debutante is being presented at Grover Cleveland's inaugural ball, while Democratic party spoilsmen look on from an antechamber.*

In 1888 the opposition returned to power committed to a high protective tariff. In the Republican campaign poster at right, Harrison promises protection to everything but polygamy, while Cleveland is presented as the foe of American industry.

"LET OUT"—BRIEFLY

My God," lamented President Cleveland, "what is there in this office that any man should ever want to get into it!" In spite of some first-term accomplishments (he had approved the Interstate Commerce Act, vetoed fraudulent pension bills, repealed the hobbling Tenure of Office Act, and instituted civil service reforms), his administration had not been happy. Party members wrangled for patronage, businessmen fought his tariff reduction proposal, and Civil War veterans resented his pension vetoes. Another political mark against him was his ill-timed gesture of conciliation toward the South. In the summer of 1887 the War Department decided it might be "a graceful act" to return to their former owners "a number of Confederate flags which the fortunes of war placed in our hands during the late Civil War." The recommendation, approved by President Cleveland, created a furor among Republicans and the already hostile veterans of the Grand Army of the Republic. Republican Foraker of Ohio declared, "No rebel flags will be surrendered while I am Governor." The commander of the G.A.R. was more virulent: "May God palsy the hand that wrote the order! May God palsy the tongue that dictated it!" The uproar forced President Cleveland to revoke the order. A shrewder politician might have anticipated the criticisms, and by tactful diplomacy, paved the way for acceptance. But Cleveland, in his straightforward manner, had again bared his breast to the enemy. Small wonder that he confided to a friend, in viewing the coming election, "I should personally like better than anything else to be let alone and let out. . . ." The voters were to grant him only a temporary reprieve. "Four years from now," said an ally after Cleveland lost to Harrison, "we mean to put you back in the White House."

THE WHOLE STORY IN A NUTSHELL!

Harrison's Ideas!

Republican Platform of 1888.

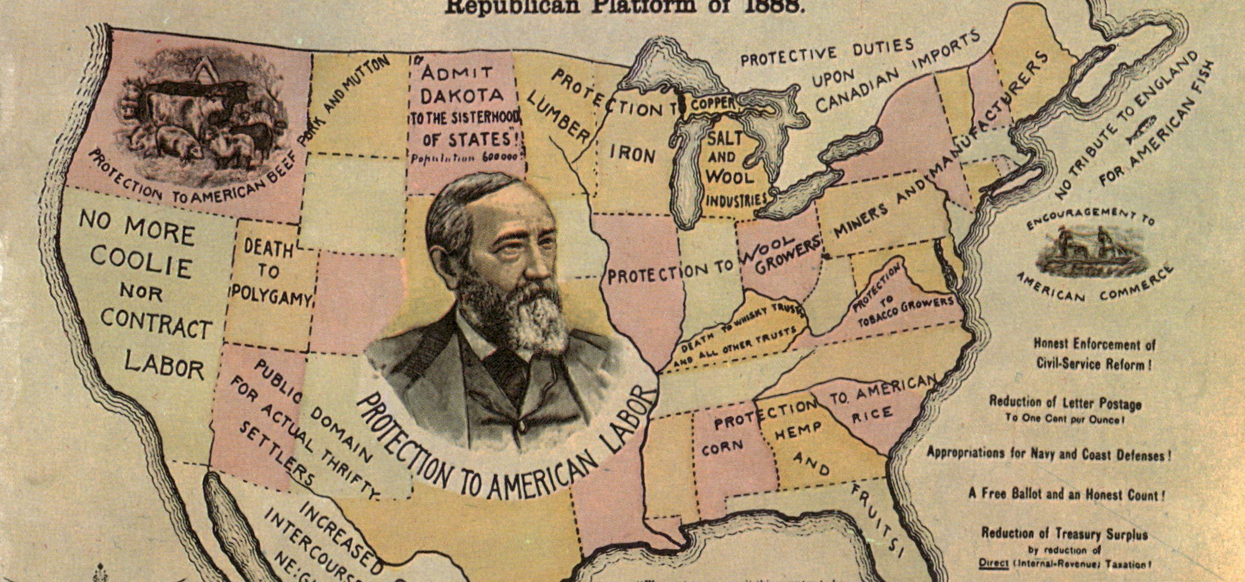

Honest Enforcement of Civil-Service Reform!

Reduction of Letter Postage To One Cent per Ounce!

Appropriations for Navy and Coast Defenses!

A Free Ballot and an Honest Count!

Reduction of Treasury Surplus by reduction of Direct (Internal-Revenue) Taxation!

Pensions for Union Soldiers!

PRICES:
10c. per Copy; $6 per Hundred; $30 per Thousand.

"We must never permit this country to become the dumping ground of the pauperism and indolence and crime of Europe. I believe that we should both protest and labor against the labor abroad, against contract labor, and against Chinese labor. Our protective system is a barrier against the flood of foreign importations and the competition of underpaid labor in Europe. Those who want to lower the dyke owe it to those who live behind it to make a plainer statement of their purposes. Do they invite the flood or do they believe in the dyke? We would have more confidence in the professions of these alleged reformers could we hear one of them occasionally say that he was a Protectionist. This is not a question of a seven-per-cent. reduction in tariff schedules; but it is a question of wide-apart principles. But let us turn from those things that are scheduled that have their places in our Census returns to those things which belong to the higher man - his spiritual and moral nature. I congratulate you not so much upon the rich farm lands of your country as upon your virtuous and happy homes. It is in the home that we first learn obedience and respect for law. Parental authority is the type of beneficent government. It is in the home that we learn to love, in the mother that bore us, that which is virtuous, consecrated and pure. I take more pride in the fact that the Republican party has always been the friend and protector of the American home than in aught else. By the beneficent Homestead Law it created more than a half million of homes, and by the Emancipation Proclamation it converted a million cattle pens into homes. And it is still true to those principles that will preserve contentment and prosperity and purity in our homes.—*BENJAMIN HARRISON.*

Cleveland's Ideas!

Fruits of "Free-Wool Message," "Mills' Bill" and General Democratic Policy.

FREE TRADE · PEACE · GOOD WILL AMONG NATIONS · Cobden Club

Seal of the Cobden Club.

"It is to the New World that the Cobden Club is chiefly looking as the most-likely sphere for its vigorous foreign policy. It has done what it can in Europe, and is now turning its eyes Westward and bracing itself for the struggle which is to come. ***It cannot rest while the United States are unsubdued.***" (!)
—From The London Daily Times, July 18, 1880.

A number of the members whom President Cleveland has called into his Cabinet, to be his *Constitutional advisers are members of this Free-Trade Cobden Club*, notably—Thos. F. Bayard, Secretary of State, and L. Q. C. Lamar, late Secretary of the Interior, now Justice of the U. S. Supreme Court. Chas. S. Fairchild, Secretary of the Treasury, and Wm. C. Endicott, Secretary of War, are also reported to be members.

"I am in favor of an amendment to the Constitution disqualifying the President from re-election. When we consider the *patronage* of this *great office*, the allurements of power, the TEMPTATION to RETAIN PUBLIC PLACE ONCE GAINED, and, more than all, the availability a party finds in an incumbent when a *horde of office-seekers*, with a zeal born of benefits received and fostered by the hope of favors yet to come, *stand ready to* ***aid with money*** and trained political service, I recognize in the *eligibility of the President for re-election* a ***most-serious danger*** to that calm, deliberate and intelligent political action which must characterize a government by the People." Cleveland's letter of acceptance Aug. 18, 1884.

"My Friends, you will never have any genuine reform in the civil service until you adopt the *one-term* principle in reference to the Presidency. So long as the incumbent can hope for a second term ***he will use*** the immense patronage of the Government to procure his renomination and secure his re-election."
Speech by Allen G. Thurman, At Columbus, O., 1872.

"I believe in Free Trade as I believe in the Protestant religion." - **Grover Cleveland.** "All trade should be free."—**Speaker Carlisle.** "I am for Free Speech, Free Men and Free Trade."—**Roger Q. Mills** (author of Mills' Bill). "The Democratic Party is a Free-Trade party or it is nothing."—**H. Watterson.** "Add to the Free List as many articles as possible."—**Secretary Fairchild** of President Cleveland's Cabinet. "It would be a glorious consummation of this debate [on Mills' Bill] could we have gentlemen on the other [Republican] side join in this invocation to clear the way for British Cobden Free Trade."—**S. S. Cox** (Democratic Congressman from N.Y.). "Mr. Mills' speech was a vigorous Free-Trade effort."-**Henry George**

Some of the Features of the Free-Trade Mills Bill, as passed by the Democratic House of Representatives, July 21, 1888:

It proposes to place upon the "Free List" more than 100 articles—chiefly the products of Northern and Western industries—that are now protected by duties, which, if removed, would result in their utter destruction!

It admits Manufactured Soap free of duty and taxes the Chemicals from which Soap is made!!

It substitutes "ad valorem" for specific duties; thereby establishing fraud and encouraging dishonesty by this means afforded British Manufacturers and Importers of making undervaluations!

It establishes a protective duty of 100¼ per cent. upon Southern Rice, while Potatoes, the great product of the farmers of the North and West are admitted free!

It affixes a duty of 45 per cent. upon Hoop Iron which is used by the North and West, while the same Hoop Iron which is used by the South for Cotton Ties is admitted free!

It strikes the rising and developing industries and those that are comparatively unorganized, like the Wool-growing industry, but dares not face the organized Sugar, Oil and Whiskey Trusts!

It places a higher duty, by 5 per cent., upon the poor man's Clothing than it does upon the rich man's Carpet!

It is a comtemptible device, which, to reduce the revenue $5,000,000 and the customs duties 8¼ cents per capita, abolishes protection from a single industry (Wool) in which 2,000,000 Northern and Western farmers are directly interested, and, at the same time, retains a revenue of $58,000,000 on Sugar (or 96¼ cents per capita), to cater to the sugar producers in the single Southern State of Louisiana, and the wealthy members of the Democratic Sugar Trust!

It frees almost every product of Northern industry and protects every product of exclusively Southern industry!

Post this in your Home, Office, Store, Club-room, Workshop or Factory.

The Puck *cartoon above illustrates the fate of the United States Treasury during the four years of Benjamin Harrison's administration. When Cleveland left office in 1889, the Treasury was swollen with a large surplus; when he returned in 1893, the surplus was depleted and the gold reserve had dropped below the danger point. In the interval the "Billion-Dollar Congress," as the fifty-first was dubbed, had managed to expend—for the first time in peacetime history—over a billion dollars in a single session. "God help the*

surplus," cried Harrison's Commissioner of Pensions "Corporal" James Tanner, whose policy was to give a grant to "every old comrade that needs it." The nation's reaction to such extravagance was manifested in the next presidential election. The cartoon shows Cleveland returning to a looted Treasury, which Harrison, in new spats and top hat, bequeaths with the comment, "The People Wanted A Change, And They Got It." To this Puck *responds, "But The Change Was Made in 1889, And We Are Still Suffering From It."*

AMERICA'S INVENTORS

ALEXANDER GRAHAM BELL

By family tradition, Alexander Graham Bell was keenly interested in acoustics—specifically, in teaching the deaf to speak. Shortly after his emigration from Scotland in 1870 he was doing just that, at a special school in Boston, and training other teachers as well. An early interest in telegraphy led him to try to develop a "speaking" model; by June of 1875 his apparatus was transmitting varied pitches, and the following March an intelligible sentence was sent and received. Bell's device changed sound into electrical current and back into sound again. Voice waves made a disk vibrate, causing interruptions in the current of a wire connected to a second disk. These variances made the second disk vibrate precisely as the first—made it "talk." The commercial possibilities were obvious: the Bell Telephone Company had to fight more than six hundred lawsuits to protect its patents. At his Volta Laboratory, Bell invented the photophone for the transmission of speech by light, and the telephone probe for locating metal objects in human bodies. He patented improvements on Edison's phonograph and made important contributions to the stability of early aircraft. Among many other positions, Bell—who became an American citizen in 1882—was president of the National Geographic Society and a regent of the Smithsonian Institution. He died in Nova Scotia in 1922.

BOTH: BROWN BROTHERS

OTTMAR MERGENTHALER

Ottmar Mergenthaler's perfection of the linotype machine was a master achievement of the Gilded Age. It made printing faster and cheaper, facilitating the mass communication so necessary in that bewilderingly fast paced era. Mergenthaler was eighteen when he emigrated from Germany in 1872; he went to work for a cousin, an instrument maker in Washington and Baltimore. Off and on for twelve years Mergenthaler experimented with machines to bypass the old methods of manual typesetting. Such machines existed, but their lines still required hand "justification" (spacing the words to make the line come out evenly), and their re-usable type tended to wear unevenly and had to be constantly re-sorted. Mergenthaler finally conceived a machine that would cast its own type. Characters would be impressed on papier-mâché strips; into these molds would go hot lead to form cast letters for printing. Eventually it was found that the lead could be remelted and cast into new type again and again. The first direct-casting machine was completed in 1884; soon it had an automatic justifier, and the New York *Tribune* put it to use. Mergenthaler quarreled with the board of directors of his printing company and resigned in 1888, but continued to make improvements on his linotype until his death in 1899. He was only forty-five when he died of tuberculosis.

MICHAEL PUPIN

A Scottish-American had invented the telephone, and in the 1890's an American of Austro-Hungarian birth perfected the means to make long-distance telephony commercially feasible. Michael Pupin knew that vibrations in a wire weighted at regular intervals did not die out as quickly as those in an "unloaded" wire. Applying this idea to sound-attenuation problems in electrical speech transmission, he developed formulas for the exact placement of "loading coils" in both underground and overhead wires. Telephone companies found that Pupin's system not only lessened distortion and sound loss, but also permitted the use of smaller and cheaper wires. An impoverished Pupin had emigrated to the United States in 1874, but nine years later he was a citizen and a graduate of Columbia University, whose faculty he joined in 1889. He was professor of electromechanics there from 1901 to 1931. Pupin made one of the earliest X-ray tubes, and after obtaining the first X-ray picture in America in January of 1896, developed a method of greatly reducing the exposure time required in X-raying. He held thirty-four different patents. Pupin was a magnetic public speaker and a prolific author whose publications ranged from scientific papers to his Pulitzer Prize-winning autobiography, *From Immigrant to Inventor*, published in 1923. He died thirteen years later.

THOMAS EDISON

In 1870 Thomas Edison sold the rights to an improved stock ticker he had designed and used the money to begin staffing an "invention factory"; during the next decade he made his mark as one of America's great inventors. In 1874 he produced a multiplex telegraph capable of sending four messages simultaneously over a single wire; in 1876 he devised a carbon telephone transmitter; a year later the phonograph was born when Edison reproduced sound with a hand-cranked, foil-wrapped cylinder and a scoring needle. He was thirty-two in 1879, the year he developed a practicable carbon filament light bulb (earlier bulbs had been too expensive). Ever alert to the commercial possibilities of his efforts, Edison worked on auxiliary equipment—generators, conductors, cables—and soon established the Pearl Street power station in New York. He later invented the mimeograph and improved upon (among others) such items as the fluoroscope, the motion-picture projector, the electric dynamo, the storage battery, and railroad signaling devices; he was hailed as "America's most useful citizen." But more and more he concentrated on organizing companies to make and sell his products. He held a total of 1,093 patents, and his frequent battles to protect them led to his remark that a patent is "simply an invitation to a lawsuit." Thomas Edison died in 1931.

Puck

"*One after the other—let the good work go on!*" *says the caption on the 1893* Puck *cartoon above. Having demolished the silver idol in the background by repealing the Sherman Silver-Purchase Act, Cleveland attacks the multilimbed trust god. But President Cleveland's axe was blunted when Congress refused to lower the tariff.*

The 1894 photograph at top right shows "Coxey's Army" on the march to Washington to petition for relief from mass unemployment. The marchers were met by Attorney General Richard Olney's police forces, who dispersed the protesters by force and violence.

A Harper's Weekly *artist made the rendition at lower right of National Guardsmen firing into an angry mob of demonstrators during the Chicago Pullman strike of 1894. Cleveland was highly criticized for sending in the troops against the wishes of Governor Altgeld.*

LIBRARY OF CONGRESS

Harper's Weekly

"A MAN OF COURAGE"

Cleveland's second administration was not, to him personally, a greater satisfaction than his first. His achievements in foreign relations—the arbitration of Venezuela's border dispute and his anti-imperialist stand on Hawaii—were largely obscured by the domestic problems following the financial panic of 1893. His heroic fight to preserve the gold standard was not fully appreciated during his administration. What was most obvious during those years was the President's mismanagement of the labor problem, particularly his severe treatment of the Chicago Pullman strikers and the unemployed protesters of "Coxey's Army." In 1897 Cleveland left office in a storm of criticism, gratefully retiring to the quiet college town of Princeton, New Jersey. The Clevelands were welcomed into the social and intellectual life of the community, and in 1901 the ex-President was elected to the university's board of trustees. He formed a lasting friendship with Andrew West, dean of the graduate school, and he was on intimate terms with the university's president, Woodrow Wilson, although his innate conservatism often clashed with the latter's progressive approach to education. He was in great demand as a speaker and in 1904 published a collection of his lectures under the title *Presidential Problems*. Before his death in 1908 he had completely regained the country's veneration. Describing the tumultuous ovation that Cleveland received on a 1903 trip to St. Louis, biographer Allan Nevins remarked, "It was the apology of the West to a man of courage." Many analysts have been disappointed in Cleveland's leadership, complaining that he was most steadfast in his protection of businessmen and that he had little sympathy for the problems of the farmer and the laborer. His friend Woodrow Wilson offered perhaps the most astute observation: "You may think Cleveland's administration was Democratic. It was not. Cleveland was a conservative Republican."

FACTS IN SUMMARY: GROVER CLEVELAND

CHRONOLOGY

UNITED STATES		CLEVELAND
Bank panic	1837	*Born March 18*
Repeal of Independent Treasury Act	1841	*Moves to Fayetteville, N.Y.*
War with Mexico	1846	
Gadsden Purchase	1853	*Teaches school*
Buchanan elected President	1856	
John Brown's raid at Harpers Ferry	1859	*Admitted to the bar*
Lincoln elected President	1860	
Civil War begins	1861	
Battle of Shiloh	1862	*Elected ward supervisor*
Emancipation Proclamation	1863	*Appointed assistant district attorney of Erie County*
Battle of Gettysburg		
Lee surrenders to Grant	1865	*Loses election for district attorney*
Lincoln assassinated		
Johnson impeached	1868	
Grant elected President		
	1870	*Elected sheriff of Erie County*
Hayes elected President	1877	
Arthur becomes President	1881	*Elected mayor of Buffalo*
	1882	*Elected governor of New York*
	1884	*Elected President*
Treasury surplus grows	1886	*Suggests reduction in tariff*
		Marries Frances Folsom
Electoral Count Act	1887	*Vetoes dependent pension bill*
Interstate Commerce Act		*Institutes repeal of Tenure of Office Act*
Hatch Act		*Urges tariff reform*
Harrison elected President	1888	*Loses bid for re-election*
Sherman Antitrust Act	1890	
Sherman Silver-Purchase Act		
McKinley Tariff		
	1891	*Writes "silver letter"*
	1892	*Re-elected President*
Bank panic	1893	*Asks repeal of Sherman Silver-Purchase Act*
		Quashes treaty for Hawaiian annexation
"Coxey's Army"	1894	*Sends troops to restore order during Pullman strike*
Gold reserve depleted	1895	*Makes deal with Morgan to solve Treasury crisis*
McKinley elected President	1896	
War with Spain	1898	
Theodore Roosevelt becomes President	1901	*Becomes Princeton University trustee*
	1908	*Dies June 24*

UNITED STATES March 4, 1893—March 4, 1897

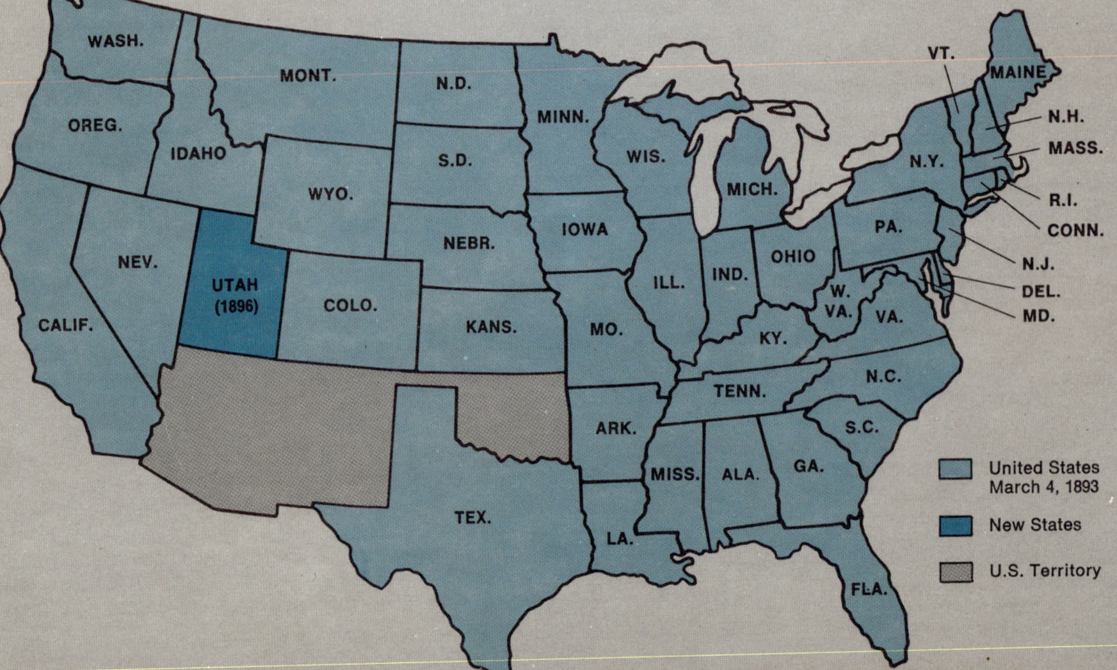

BIOGRAPHICAL FACTS

BIRTH: Caldwell, N.J., March 18, 1837

ANCESTRY: Irish-English

FATHER: Richard Falley Cleveland; b. Norwich, Conn., June 19, 1804; d. Holland Patent, N.Y., Oct. 1, 1853

FATHER'S OCCUPATION: Minister

MOTHER: Ann Neal Cleveland; b. Baltimore, Md., Feb. 4, 1806; d. Holland Patent, N.Y., July 19, 1882

BROTHERS: William Neal (1832–1906); Richard Cecil (1835–1872); Lewis Frederick (1841–1872)

SISTERS: Anna Neal (1830–1909); Mary Allen (1833–1914); Margaret Louise (1838–1932); Susan Sophia (1843–?); Rose (1846–1918)

WIFE: Frances Folsom; b. Buffalo, N.Y., July 21, 1864; d. Oct. 29, 1947

MARRIAGE: Washington, D.C., June 2, 1886

CHILDREN: Ruth (1891–1904); Esther (1893–); Marion (1895–); Richard Folsom (1897–); Francis Grover (1903–)

EDUCATION: Public schools

RELIGIOUS AFFILIATION: Presbyterian

OCCUPATION BEFORE PRESIDENCY: Lawyer

PRE-PRESIDENTIAL OFFICES: Erie County Assistant District Attorney; Sheriff of Erie County; Mayor of Buffalo; Governor of New York

AGE AT INAUGURATION: 47

OCCUPATION AFTER PRESIDENCY: Princeton University trustee

DEATH: Princeton, N.J., June 24, 1908

PLACE OF BURIAL: Princeton, N.J.

ELECTION OF 1884

CANDIDATES	ELECTORAL VOTE	POPULAR VOTE
Grover Cleveland Democratic	219	4,879,507
James G. Blaine Republican	182	4,850,293
Benjamin F. Butler Greenback-Labor	—	175,370
John P. St. John Prohibition	—	150,369

FIRST ADMINISTRATION

INAUGURATION: March 4, 1885; the Capitol, Washington, D.C.

VICE PRESIDENT: Thomas A. Hendricks

SECRETARY OF STATE: Thomas F. Bayard

SECRETARY OF THE TREASURY: Daniel Manning; Charles S. Fairchild (from April 1, 1887)

SECRETARY OF WAR: William C. Endicott

ATTORNEY GENERAL: Augustus H. Garland

POSTMASTER GENERAL: William F. Vilas; Don M. Dickinson (from Jan. 16, 1888)

SECRETARY OF THE NAVY: William C. Whitney

SECRETARY OF THE INTERIOR: Lucius Q. C. Lamar; William F. Vilas (from Jan. 16, 1888)

SECRETARY OF AGRICULTURE: Norman J. Colman

SUPREME COURT APPOINTMENTS: Lucius Q. C. Lamar (1888); Melville W. Fuller, Chief Justice (1888)

49th CONGRESS (March 4, 1885–March 4, 1887):
Senate: 43 Republicans; 34 Democrats
House: 183 Democrats; 140 Republicans; 2 Others

50th CONGRESS (March 4, 1887–March 4, 1889):
Senate: 39 Republicans; 37 Democrats
House: 169 Democrats; 152 Republicans; 4 Others

END OF PRESIDENTIAL TERM: March 4, 1889

ELECTION OF 1892

CANDIDATES	ELECTORAL VOTE	POPULAR VOTE
Grover Cleveland Democratic	277	5,555,426
Benjamin Harrison Republican	145	5,182,690
James B. Weaver People's	22	1,029,846
John Bidwell Prohibition	—	264,133
Simon Wing Socialist Labor	—	21,164

SECOND ADMINISTRATION

INAUGURATION: March 4, 1893; the Capitol, Washington, D.C.

VICE PRESIDENT: Adlai E. Stevenson

SECRETARY OF STATE: Walter Q. Gresham; Richard Olney (from June 10, 1895)

SECRETARY OF THE TREASURY: John G. Carlisle

SECRETARY OF WAR: Daniel S. Lamont

ATTORNEY GENERAL: Richard Olney; Judson Harmon (from June 11, 1895)

POSTMASTER GENERAL: Wilson S. Bissell; William L. Wilson (from April 4, 1895)

SECRETARY OF THE NAVY: Hilary A. Herbert

SECRETARY OF THE INTERIOR: Hoke Smith; David R. Francis (from Sept. 4, 1896)

SECRETARY OF AGRICULTURE: Julius Sterling Morton

SUPREME COURT APPOINTMENTS: Edward D. White (1894); Rufus W. Peckham (1895)

53rd CONGRESS (March 4, 1893–March 4, 1895):
Senate: 44 Democrats; 38 Republicans; 3 Others
House: 218 Democrats; 127 Republicans; 11 Others

54th CONGRESS (March 4, 1895–March 4, 1897):
Senate: 43 Republicans; 39 Democrats; 6 Others
House: 244 Republicans; 105 Democrats; 7 Others

STATE ADMITTED: Utah (1896)

END OF PRESIDENTIAL TERM: March 4, 1897

BENJAMIN HARRISON HOME

THE TWENTY-THIRD PRESIDENT (1889–1893)

BENJAMIN HARRISON

A month after the national election of 1888, Republican National Committee Chairman Matt Quay journeyed to Indianapolis to discuss Cabinet choices with President-elect Benjamin Harrison. Although Harrison had received nearly one hundred thousand fewer votes than his opponent, incumbent Grover Cleveland, he had managed to capture an electoral majority, and he was grateful. "Providence," he said as he greeted Quay, "has given us the victory." For the moment the chairman held his tongue, but later, as he repeated the conversation to a colleague, he remarked, "Think of the man! He ought to know that Providence hadn't a damn thing to do with it."

What had given the Republicans the victory was a combination of good organization and corruption. They bought the votes they needed to win in one of the key states, Harrison's own Indiana. In another crucial state, Cleveland's New York, they dealt and bribed their way into an affiliation with Tammany Hall, which was only too glad to devote its machinery to the defeat of the hated reformer from Buffalo. Such dealings were not too difficult, for this was the era some historians have called "The Period of No Decision" in the United States. It was a time when the nation was converting with incredible speed from an agrarian to an urban-industrial culture, when neither party faced up to the growing labor problems of the expanding cities or to the increasing discontent of the farmer. It was a time when the American people and their leaders enjoyed little or no rapport, when many citizens—not through apathy, but with considerable justice—simply did not care which party was in power; some joined splinter parties; the more cynical put their votes up for sale, cheap. Coldly dignified, honest, but absolutely colorless, Benjamin Harrison was proud of his country's industrial growth but un-

This portrait of Benjamin Harrison hangs near one of his grandfather, William Henry, in the Harrison Memorial Home in Indiana.

BENJAMIN HARRISON HOME

This lithograph of Harrison's birthplace at North Bend, Ohio, was made from an oil painting done in 1840.

responsive to the social problems it created. He was above all else a party man, and in those days Republicans regarded party loyalty as tantamount to patriotism. Once he found himself in the office that Providence (and/or Matt Quay) had given him, however, he sincerely tried to do the job. He willingly sacrificed his own popularity and the trust of his party, but he was just the wrong man in the wrong place at the wrong time. As Acting Attorney General William Howard Taft put it in 1890: "The President is not popular with the members of either house. His manner of treating them is not at all fortunate, and when they have an interview with him they generally come away mad. . . . I think this is exceedingly unfortunate, because I am sure we have never had a man in the White House who was more conscientiously seeking to do his duty."

Benjamin Harrison had had a political apprenticeship the equal of which few men could boast. Service to the nation was in his genes: his great-grandfather, also named Benjamin Harrison, had been a signer of the Declaration of Independence; his grandfather, William Henry Harrison, had been a military hero, congressman, senator, diplomat, and, briefly, President of the United States; his father, John S. Harrison, had been a member of the House of Representatives. (Indeed, the Harrison family's record of participation in government is equaled by few in the United States; a twentieth-century William Henry Harrison, grandson of the twenty-third President, has served as a congressman from Wyoming several times since 1951.)

Benjamin Harrison was born on August 20, 1833, on his grandfather's estate at North Bend, Ohio, not far from Cincinnati. He was the second son born to John Scott and Elizabeth Irwin Harrison, but he grew up with two older half sisters, children of his father's earlier marriage. Both scholarly and athletic, young Harrison had a private tutor but attended the country school as well.

Although Scott Harrison was hard hit by recurring bad times in the forties, he sent Benjamin and another son to Farmers' College in Cincinnati in 1847. After three years, Benjamin transferred to Ohio's Miami University, the "Yale of the West." He graduated with distinction in 1852 and the next year married a girl he had met there, Caroline Scott. After two years of law studies with a firm in Cincinnati, Harrison moved with his wife to the growing city of Indianapolis.

Of his early days in the Hoosier capital Harrison later recalled, "They were close times. . . . A $5 bill was an event." Steadily, however, the young lawyer began to make a name for himself. A neighbor, Dr. John M. Kitchen, remembered Harrison as "kindly, agreeable and studious, reserved even then, but attracting persons to him by his intellectual qualities. He was a man of notably clear character and made a success of everything he undertook. . . . I do not think he ever had an acquaintance with anyone that ripened into the hottest kind of friendship."

In early 1855, William Wallace, a young attorney with political ambitions, approached Harrison and proposed that they become partners. For Wallace it meant freedom to campaign for the office of clerk of Marion County without neglecting his growing practice, and for Harrison it meant the clientele he had lacked. Wallace lost the election, but the partnership endured, and after one year the firm was among the most prominent and prosperous in Indianapolis.

Back in Ohio, John Scott Harrison had been twice elected (in 1852 and 1854) to the United States House of Representatives. Although he was a dedicated and hard-working Whig congressman, the elder Harrison had little good to say about the political profession, admonishing his son to stay away from it, from its many "temptations" and "many inducements to stray from the proper path." Nevertheless, Benjamin Harrison was attracted to politics, and to the distress of his father, joined the newly formed Republican party. In 1857 he ran successfully for the office of Indianapolis city attorney and in 1860 became state supreme court reporter.

In July, 1862, when enthusiasm for the Civil War had ebbed, Governor Oliver P. Morton asked Harrison to recruit men for the 70th Indiana Volunteers. Harrison did so and was made colonel of the regiment, which was dispatched to Kentucky to guard the Louisville and Nashville Railroad. He soon realized that his men were soldiers in name only and began to prepare them for battle. There are some men who can apply discipline sternly and retain the respect and even the affection of their men; Harrison was not one of them. His icy coldness and abruptness made him one of the less popular brigade commanders. Still, his record was good, and the performance of his men during the Atlanta Campaign proved his abilities. By the war's end he was a brigadier general.

After the war Harrison returned to his practice and almost immediately became one of the most sought-after lawyers in Indiana. He had a superb memory, the ability to analyze and make sense of a mass of facts and figures at a glance, and a knack for making eloquent, expressive presentations in court. If he was aloof in public, he was affectionate and good-natured at home, devoted to his wife and two children. In appearance he was short—about five feet seven inches—red-bearded, blue-eyed, and fair; his stocky frame moved quickly and was generally attired fashionably.

Although the retired general did not immediately re-enter politics, he remained interested in public affairs and was particularly active in philanthropic activities. He was a religious man: an elder in the Presbyterian church, he taught a Bible class for men and

LIBRARY OF CONGRESS

The photograph above, taken when Harrison was in college, indicates his early fondness for beards.

was superintendent of a Sunday school. Then, in 1872, Harrison received some support for the Republican nomination for governor of Indiana, but Governor Oliver Morton blocked him. Morton, it seemed, was afraid that Harrison's candidacy "would lift him into dangerous prominence." Four years later, however, when the regular Republican candidate was exposed by the Democrats as having a corrupt record, the Republicans replaced him on their ticket with the highly regarded Harrison. In a hard-fought campaign, Harrison lost to James Douglas Williams, although he ran ahead of the ticket throughout the state.

In 1880, Harrison, who was the chairman of the Indiana delegation to the Republican National Convention, was instrumental in securing the presidential nomination for James A. Garfield. Garfield offered him a Cabinet post, but Harrison had been elected that same year to the United States Senate, where he preferred to serve.

BENJAMIN HARRISON HOME

"Harrison, by God, I'll make you a Brigadier for this fight," said Joe Hooker during the Atlanta Campaign; and in 1865 Harrison was promoted.

Until this point in his career, Benjamin Harrison was notable for his independence, professional competence, and intelligence. He had been, from the start, a good, steady, dependable Republican, but he had not been predictable. A radical in the matter of Reconstruction during Andrew Johnson's ill-fated administration, he had at the same time been a conservative in economic matters. Governor Morton had objected to Harrison's resistance to being "handled." But Hoosier Republicans were disunited, and Harrison, committed to no one faction, seemed just the man to unite the party. When he announced that he would like a Senate seat (legislatures at that time elected senators), the Republican Indiana legislature responded favorably, for Harrison had earned its support.

Having taken his Senate seat, Harrison retained his independence. While generally aligning himself with the moderate wing of his party (the "Half-Breeds"), he remained a fiscal conservative. He favored the programs Republicans favored but favored them only to what he thought was a "reasonable" extent: he was for a protective tariff, so long as it was reasonable; he supported reasonable labor legislation, reasonable railroad regulation, reasonable pensions for veterans. If he departed from the norm at all, it was, to his credit, usually a humanitarian departure. He was, for example, sympathetic to the problems of the Indians and the homesteaders and defied his big-money-dominated party by supporting legislation protecting them from the railroads; and he voted against the Chinese exclusion bill (apparently on constitutional grounds).

During the first Cleveland administration, the Democrats, who had finally pulled alongside the Republicans in national strength, gained control of the Indiana legislature, gerrymandered the state, and defeated Harrison's effort to retain his Senate seat in 1886.

Early in 1888 James G. Blaine announced from Europe that he would not be a candidate for the Presidency again, despite the fact that Cleveland's unpopular tariff made him an eminently beatable opponent. Many of Blaine's supporters rallied behind Harrison, but they had a difficult time convincing him that he was responsible for publicizing his own candidacy. Finally, on Washington's Birthday, he traveled to Detroit, where he more or less officially declared himself available. Before the Michigan Club, he said: "I am a dead statesman ["*No! No!*" protested the audience], but I am a living and a rejuvenated Republican. . . ." The speech was given national press coverage, was called "one of his greatest" orations, and made the expression "rejuvenated Republicanism" the catch phrase of the Harrison drive for the nomination. In a Chicago speech four weeks later, he recalled his Civil War experiences and reminded the nation that the Republican party had taken "the ship of state when there was treachery at the helm, when there was mutiny on the deck, when the ship was among the rocks, and we put loyalty at the helm. . . ." From then on he was General Harrison to the nation—the war-hero grandson of Old Tippecanoe.

At the Chicago convention the presence of James G. Blaine, who was in Scotland, was nevertheless felt. Through the first several ballots, favorite-son candidates were not withdrawn, for the delegates were waiting to hear from Blaine. Then word came from Scotland: Blaine wanted Harrison. He was nominated on the eighth ballot. His running mate was Levi P. Morton of New York.

The American people spoke, but the electoral college spoke louder, and Benjamin Harrison, who received some 90,000 fewer votes than Cleveland, was elected President of the United States. On their way to victory the Republicans contracted so many debts that the possibility of clean-slate ad-

NEW-YORK HISTORICAL SOCIETY

This campaign kerchief shows how determinedly the Republicans meant to protect "infant industries."

ministration was all but destroyed. Harrison had made civil service reform a major campaign issue, but once installed in the White House, he could not follow through on his pledges. The bulk of the Republican party's four-million-dollar campaign fund had been supplied through the influence and intervention of John Wanamaker, the "merchant prince" of Philadelphia. Wanamaker was rewarded with the Postmaster Generalship, and although Harrison had said that "only the interest of the public service should suggest removals from office," Wanamaker permitted the removal of all the Democrats in his department—thirty thousand in the first year. The President even suspended civil service guidelines established by Cleveland, replaced Democratic officeholders with Republicans, and then reinstated the rules. And yet Harrison's meager efforts to reform the service were enough to earn the animosity of Quay and many other Republican regulars, though not nearly enough to win friends among the reformers.

Part of the Republican strategy during the campaign had been to concentrate in the doubtful states on Civil War veterans, who were numerous enough to swing the vote to Harrison. The strategy had worked principally because the Republicans had pledged liberal pensions. Harrison made good the pledge by appointing James Tanner pension commissioner. Interpreting existing legislation in the most liberal manner, Tanner doled out millions more Treasury dollars than had Cleveland's commissioner, and as though that were not enough, Congress passed in 1890 a pension act that awarded still more liberal benefits to veterans (anyone who had served in the Union army ninety days or more qualified) unable to do manual labor—regardless of the cause of disability. Therefore, almost any veteran suffering from old age was eligible. Widows, orphans, and dependent parents of veterans were also given pensions.

In some respects President Harrison was sensitively tuned to his times; in others he was impervious to them. The Industrial Revolution had given way to the Industrial Age; Harrison knew that business—from the gathering of raw materials to manufacturing, distribution, financing, and international trade—was now responsible for the health and wealth of the country. He understood that business was leading the United States—and the other great powers of the world—toward an age of imperialism, and he was proud of the big new Navy and merchant marine fleets being built under Secretary of the Navy Benjamin F. Tracy. But there were social problems that Harrison did not—or could not—appreciate.

BROWN BROTHERS

First there was the farmer, trying to hold on to his disappearing way of life. The railroads had opened up the width of the continent; by the end of the Civil War, homesteaders farmed the soil from ocean to ocean. But from that point onward, American economics had become industry- and urban-oriented. In 1887, when the land-speculation boom was halted by drought, insects, an early frost, and dollar deflation, the *Progressive Farmer*, a North Carolina journal, noted that there was "a screw loose" in America's new industrial economy: "The railroads have never been so prosperous, and yet agriculture languishes. . . . Towns and cities flourish and 'boom' . . . and yet agriculture languishes. Salaries and fees were never so temptingly high and desirable, and yet agriculture languishes."

Then there was the laborer, who represented the wave of the future. Harrison's administration was part of that incredible period (1880–1910) during which eighteen million immigrants entered the United States. These people not only helped form the great labor class in the United States; their continuing arrival created a gigantic labor issue, for many American workers feared their competition.

It was this great mass of Americans—farmers and laborers—that the administration (indeed, both political parties) ignored.

Hawaii's Queen Liliuokalani (left) opposed American annexation of her kingdom in the early 1890's.

And it was the realization among the people that they were being ignored that created "The Period of No Decision." There was simply nothing for the voters to choose from, nothing in government on which to decide. Harrison did not create this era or its problems, but he did typify the government mentality that avoided the problems and allowed them to smolder for years to come.

And yet the politicians knew that the farmers and workers existed. During the election campaign of 1888 both parties had pledged to do something about the control of trusts and monopolies. In 1890 Congress passed (almost unanimously) the Sherman Antitrust Act, which gave the federal courts power to prevent "conspiracy, in restraint of trade or commerce" and made the forming of a monopoly or "attempt to monopolize" a crime. The trouble with this bill was that "trust" and "monopoly" were never really defined. Ironically, the act was employed most effectively against labor unions.

Even if the Sherman Antitrust Act had actually been intended as corporation-control legislation—which it had not—the administration more than offset its passage by supporting the McKinley Tariff. Drafted by Representative William McKinley of Ohio, the tariff raised duties on dry goods and foodstuffs but removed the rates on sugar (to the benefit of the Sugar Trust). Moreover, it maintained a low tariff on the raw-material imports needed by the iron and steel industries. Prices were raised throughout the country; the consumer outcry was frantic but futile.

The Farmers' Alliances, a union of farm groups that was the forerunner of the Populist party, had long held that the deflation that had cost the farmer so much could be reversed by the free and unlimited coinage of silver. (It was argued, probably correctly, that free silver—regulated by the government, not banks—would stabilize the price of silver and keep much more money in circulation, thus inflating the dollar.) The Bland-Allison Act of 1878 had provided for some silver coinage, but for the most part, American bank notes were based on a gold standard. When, in 1889, the omnibus bill admitted Montana, Washington, and the Dakotas to the Union, the Farmers' Alliances' strength was increased in Congress; and in June, 1890, the Senate passed a free silver coinage bill, but the House blocked its passage. The Westerners then threatened to vote against the McKinley Tariff, which was pending at the same time, and finally negotiated a compromise with the Eastern conservatives: the tariff and the Sherman Silver-Purchase Act were both passed. While not providing for unlimited silver coinage, the silver act did require the Treasury to purchase 4,500,000 ounces of silver monthly and made bank notes payable in gold or silver at the discretion of the Treasury. But, because financiers were afraid of the effects of the act and would not loosen money, deflation was unchecked and nothing was proved.

If Benjamin Harrison's role in these affairs seems understated, it is because his role was in fact small. He had filled his Cabinet with businessmen, and the Republican National Committee seemed to run the government. Though he was not successful at civil service reform, his attempts annoyed Matt Quay and Thomas Brackett Reed of Maine (the "Czar" of the House of Representatives), both of whom helped form an anti-Harrison wing in the party. Reed, despite occasional opposition from the President, continued to encourage lavish spending; Harrison's administration saw the first peacetime "Billion-Dollar Congress."

"A statesman," Reed is supposed to have said, "is a successful politician who is dead." Nevertheless, it was in the field of foreign affairs that the almost politically dead Harrison established his most statesmanly record. James G. Blaine, his Secretary of State, concentrated on bettering Pan-American relations. His most notable achievement was the formation of the International Bureau of American Republics—later renamed the Pan-American Union. Harrison not only supported Blaine in all his policies but often had to implement them himself, for the Secretary of State was ill during much of his term.

Harrison also coped wisely with two international incidents. In 1890 eleven suspected Mafia members were held, acquitted, and then lynched for the murder of the New Orleans police chief who had been investigating the Black Hand. Italy protested (three of the victims were Italian nationals) and could not understand the State Department's explanation that the affair was the province of the state of Louisiana, not of the federal government. The Italians removed their minister from the United States; the American ambassador left Italy; but Harrison concluded the incident with the payment of $25,000 to the Italian government.

During the Chilean civil war of 1891, the United States temporarily held a rebel vessel in San Diego, where it had picked up an arms shipment. Although the vessel was soon released, Chilean resentment toward the United States was high. In October a group of American sailors was attacked by a mob in Valparaiso, and two were killed. A series of indignant notes were exchanged, each demanding an apology for the last. On January 25, 1892, Harrison ended the matter by asking Congress, in so many words, for a declaration of war. Chile promptly apologized and paid an indemnity of $75,000.

The manifest destiny theory of American expansion was briefly, and unsuccessfully, reborn in the Harrison administration. When Queen Liliuokalani of Hawaii ascended to the throne in 1891, she renounced the pro-American constitution of 1887 and assumed autocratic power. American planter Sanford Dole and United States Minister John L. Stevens ordered Marines to be landed to "protect" American property. Without authorization from the State Department, Stevens recognized the "revolutionary" administration of Dole, took over the government buildings, and declared the islands an American protectorate. Harrison acknowledged the treaty of annexation, but the Senate did nothing about it. President Cleveland later withdrew it.

The Democrats had gained overwhelming control of the House of Representatives in the election of 1890. Yet, two years later, the prospect of winning re-election seemed not impossible to Harrison. The Democrats had nominated Cleveland again, but the outcome of the election was unpredictable because of the new Populist party. With some help from city labor groups, the farmers were finally in open revolt. They created a platform demanding free coinage of silver, a government-controlled flexible currency system, a graduated income tax, immigration restriction, prohibition of land ownership by aliens, public ownership of telegraphs, telephones, and railroads, an eight-hour workday for laborers, and the direct election of senators. The Populist candidate, James B. Weaver, had little chance of winning; yet it was obvious that the Populists were strong and that their votes, added to the total of either major party candidate, would probably produce victory.

After a quiet, unexciting campaign, Cleveland won by almost four hundred thousand votes and by an electoral count of 277 to 145. The Populists received over a million votes and were soon absorbed into the Democratic party.

Benjamin Harrison returned to his Indianapolis law practice, wrote a great deal, and remained a moderate voice in his party's affairs. In 1899 he accepted a commission from Venezuela and became its chief counsel in a boundary dispute with Great Britain. He worked on the case for two years, and while he was delivering his twenty-five-hour-long closing argument before the arbitration tribunal in Paris, the English representative is said to have sent a message preparing his superiors for a judgment favorable to Venezuela.

In his last years, Harrison spoke out often on the subject of the obligations of the wealthy and became more dubious about the wisdom of imperialism. In 1896 he had married a niece of his wife's (who had died in 1892). He was still healthy and vigorous and enjoyed once again the pleasures of fatherhood; his daughter was born in 1897. Then, in 1901, he contracted pneumonia and died at Indianapolis on March 13.

—DAVID JACOBS

Benj Harrison

A PICTURE PORTFOLIO

J. DOYLE DEWITT COLLECTION

Thomas Nast introduced the elephant and the donkey in the 1870's, but both parties still experimented with symbols. In 1888 the old Democratic rooster was crowing for the G.O.P.

BOTH: J. DOYLE DEWITT COLLECTION

During the presidential campaign of 1888 a voter could reflect the candidates' current relative popularity or predict the outcome of the race by tipping the above scale in favor of Harrison (the figurine at left) or Cleveland. A majority chose Cleveland, but Harrison won the electoral vote, nevertheless.

Harrison was not above using family associations to make political hay. Covers of writing tablets, such as the one at left from the 1892 campaign, gave top billing to William H. Harrison, hero of Tippecanoe; beneath the President and Mrs. Harrison are their children, Russell and Mary Harrison McKee. William Henry had been a successful "log cabin" candidate, so in 1888 his grandson used mock log cabins (below) as his campaign headquarters.

"THE ELECTION EXPENSES"

"Parties are not built up by deportment, or by ladies' magazines, or gush!" said Roscoe Conkling. Parties were organized—and maintained—by machines whose wheels were oiled by a constant flow of cash; if Benjamin Harrison ever doubted that fact he became aware of its veracity when he assumed the Presidency. He was nominated by the Republicans because he was an inoffensive lawyer from a crucial state—Indiana—with a solid military and political background. But when the machine began to move, Harrison was the passenger, not the driver. Big business, faced with tariff reductions should Cleveland be re-elected, was a natural ally, so the Republicans were able to "put the manufacturers . . . under the fire and fry all the fat out of them." The campaign fund manager was W. W. Dudley, who, it was said, had no peer "in the effective use of money for the purchase of purchasable votes. . . ." Matt Quay bargained for the support of the Knights of Labor; some manufacturers threatened their workers with unemployment should Harrison lose. In critical New York Democratic leaders were wooed and won. "Migrations" of voters to Indiana were facilitated by Pennsylvania Railroad freight trains. When the British minister foolishly told an inquirer who claimed to be an English-born naturalized American to vote for Cleveland, the advice was published and the Irish vote went solidly for Harrison. (The diplomat had been duped, but it was too late for the Democrats to do anything about it.) "When I came into power," Harrison was to reflect, "I found that the party managers had taken it all to themselves. . . . They had sold out every place to pay the election expenses."

BENJAMIN HARRISON HOME

LIBRARY OF CONGRESS

LEVI P. MORTON

Levi P. Morton was a Wall Street banker with a scant six years' experience in politics when he received the Republican vice presidential nomination in 1888. The son of a Vermont pastor, he had entered business as a storekeeper in New Hampshire, became head of a New York wholesale house in 1855, and established his own banking firm eight years later. An eminently successful businessman, he was soon an international figure in the world of finance. In 1879, at the age of fifty-five, he entered politics as a United States representative from New York. After one term he was offered the Republican nomination for the Vice Presidency but declined on the advice of Senator Roscoe Conkling. Upon Garfield's election, however, he was appointed minister to France, where his diplomatic duties during four years included the acceptance of Bartholdi's Statue of Liberty. Defeated for the Senate in 1885 and 1887, he accepted the party's second offer of the Vice Presidency in 1888. Elected to office with Harrison, he presided over the Senate for four years with scrupulous fairness and nonpartisan objectivity. In 1895 he became governor of New York. An advocate of civil service reform, he governed ably and independently, resisting all efforts of domination by Thomas C. Platt and New York's other party bosses. Resigning from office in 1897, he returned to business and established the Morton Trust Company.

"GOD HELP THE SURPLUS!"

The ideal, or even my own ideal," said President Benjamin Harrison at his inaugural, "I shall probably not attain." His candid remark proved to be an understatement. During Grover Cleveland's administration the Republicans had been the "outs" for the first time since 1861, and the party's leaders were famished for the spoils denied them. "God help the Surplus!" cried Pension Commissioner James Tanner, and soon Congress passed a sixty-million-dollar-a-year disability act benefiting—as one jubilant ex-soldier put it—all veterans "whose conditions of health are not practically perfect." New lords meant new thanes, and heads rolled in all departments overseen by members of Harrison's "Businessmen's Cabinet." Theodore Roosevelt of New York was appointed to the Civil Service Commission, but his efforts at reform were continually frustrated, and he referred to the President as "the little grey man." J. P. Morgan blithely organized his gentlemen's agreement among the railroad barons, although, as historian Matthew Josephson has written, "the ink had scarcely dried on the Interstate Commerce Act." Despite sweeping off-year election gains by the Democrats, the Speaker of the House, "Czar" Thomas Reed of Maine, maintained an iron-fisted rule. When Democratic congressmen, trying to prevent a quorum, would not answer roll calls, Reed had their names recorded as "present and refusing to vote." Reed also killed a sorely needed White House renovation and rebuilding bill advocated by Mrs. Harrison because the President had failed to appoint a Reed man to a collectorship in Portland, Maine.

LIBRARY OF CONGRESS

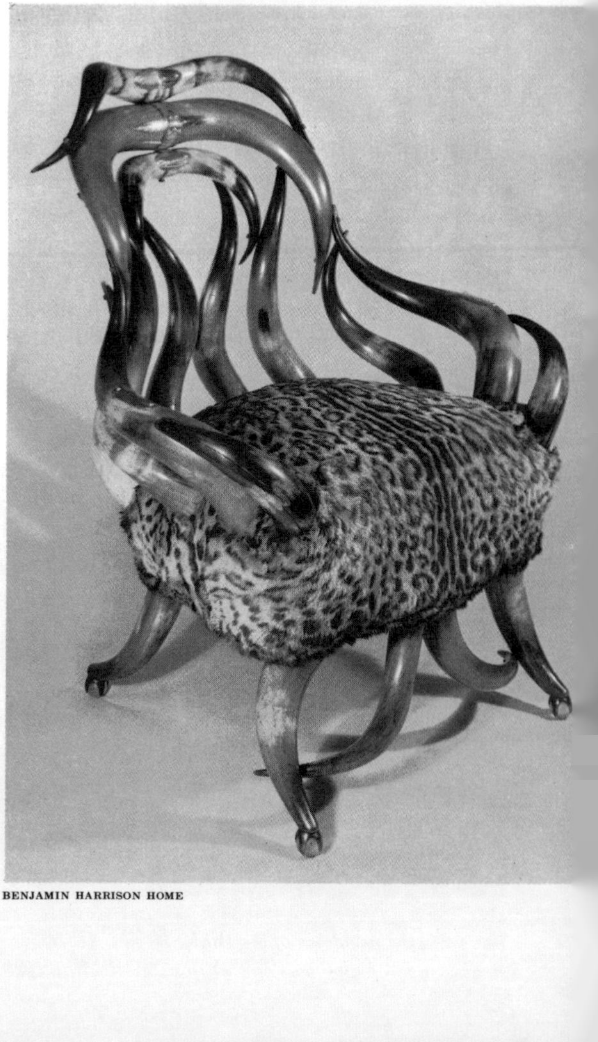

BENJAMIN HARRISON HOME

At top right is a photograph of the First Lady, Caroline Scott Harrison, who died in the White House in 1892. Below her is a steer-horn chair that was presented to Harrison as a gift. His name is spelled out on its back in small diamonds.

Far from the problems of the White House, Harrison poses (above) with the bag from a day's duckhunting. The stogie in his hand was not atypic; an Indianapolis tobacconist kept the President supplied with cigars.

CULVER PICTURES

TERENCE V. POWDERLY

Terence V. Powderly led the Knights of Labor from 1879 to 1893, when the group rose and fell as the nation's mightiest labor organization. A reformer fired by liberal concepts instilled by prior union activity in his native Pennsylvania, Powderly advocated government control of monopolies and trusts and government ownership of public utilities. He urged currency reform and felt the wage system should be supplanted by workers' cooperatives that would "own and operate mines, factories, and railroads." Although the Knights officially shunned strikes and violence (preferring arbitration), membership in the mid-eighties grew to 729,000 on the strength of successful railroad strikes. Other strikes were failures, however, and the collapse of an eight-hour-day movement in Chicago and public disapproval of the Haymarket Massacre led to the decline of the Knights' influence. Powderly, who had been called a Communist by the conservative press, served three terms as mayor of Scranton on the Greenback-Labor ticket, but by 1894 he supported the Republican party and in 1897 became commissioner general of immigration under McKinley. From 1907 until 1921, three years before he died, he headed the Division of Information of the Immigration Bureau. Powderly wrote *Thirty Years of Labor, 1859–1889* and the autobiographical *The Path I Trod.*

FOGG ART MUSEUM

CHARLES WILLIAM ELIOT

A college, said Charles William Eliot, is "a place to which a young man *is sent*"; a university, one "to which he *goes*." In 1869 Eliot became Harvard's twenty-second president, and for the next forty years he guided his alma mater's growth into one of the world's great universities. When he took office there were about sixty teachers and a thousand students; at his retirement there were six hundred and four thousand, respectively, and endowment had increased tenfold to over twenty million dollars. To the graduate complex had been added the schools of Arts and Sciences, Applied Sciences, and Business Administration. Graduate standards had been raised, notably in the Law and Medical schools. Emphasizing self-reliance, Eliot installed the elective system of undergraduate course selection. He also established a professorial exchange program and introduced the sabbatical leave. Out of Eliot's encouragement of higher education for women came Radcliffe College, founded in 1894. A firm advocate of improved pre-college education, Eliot served as chairman of the National Education Association's Committee on Secondary School Studies and helped to organize the Board of College Entrance Examinations in 1901. President Eliot wrote widely on education, political science, and religion, and edited the *Harvard Classics*, a fifty-volume home library.

CULVER PICTURES

BOOKER T. WASHINGTON

When Booker T. Washington dined with Teddy Roosevelt at the White House in 1910, a Southern newspaper called it "a crime equal to treason." Washington, typically modest, said, "Mr. Roosevelt simply found he could spare the time best during and after the dinner hour. . . ." Twenty years earlier, the ex-slave had helped found a Negro normal school at Tuskegee, Alabama, beginning, as he recalled it, with "a dilapidated shanty" and forty pupils. The institute had grown and would continue to grow; when Washington died in 1915 his teaching and public relations efforts had developed a community of over a hundred buildings (many student-built) on nearly thirty thousand acres with an endowment of almost two million dollars. Washington had toiled in salt furnaces and coal mines as a boy in West Virginia; eventually he worked his way through Hampton Institute, graduating in 1875. By the mid-1890's he was the leader of the American Negro community, always stressing pacific paths—industrial education and self-improvement—to gaining the franchise. Denounced as an "Uncle Tom" by radical Negroes, he realistically held that, at the time, "agitation of questions of social equality is the extremist folly." The most famous of his many books are *Up From Slavery* and *My Larger Education*, and a biography of Frederick Douglass.

BROWN BROTHERS

SAMUEL GOMPERS

In 1877, after seeing fellow New York City cigar makers fail in a disjointed strike to improve their lot, Samuel Gompers began to weld his trade's many unions into a single organization. An official hierarchy was established; increased dues resulted in a permanent union fund; fringe benefits were planned. The union was a prototype: by 1886 other skilled-worker groups had united internally and joined the cigar makers. Gompers would be president of this American Federation of Labor continuously, except for 1895, until his death in 1924. Born in a London tenement, Gompers was a pragmatist: he sought higher wages and shorter hours "to increase the workingman's welfare year by year." Solidarity was the keystone. Gompers felt that there should be only one union for each American trade—and with no "dual unionism" there could be no pool of strikebreakers to thwart A.F. of L. demands for concessions. Gompers did not agree with those who thought labor could eventually take over management, and this attitude enabled him to negotiate successfully with capitalists. During World War I, Gompers organized the War Committee on Labor, having already been a member of President Wilson's Council of National Defense. Gompers' two-volume *Seventy Years of Life and Labor* remains a significant account of the American labor movement.

THE WHEELS STOP

When Benjamin Harrison finally began to assert his executive authority, he contributed inevitably to a party schism. He saw to Quay's ouster from the Republican National Committee, and when J. S. Clarkson, "headsman" of the Postal Department, retired, Harrison sharply increased the number of civil servants under the merit system. His resurgent probity—and his cold, pious manner—were branded "Sunday-school politics" by Quay, who, with boss Thomas Platt, formed an anti-Harrison wing. As H. L. Stoddard, a journalist, noted: "No threats are made, no open opposition shown, but the President suddenly discovers that the wheels are not turning. . . . Nominees are not confirmed . . . departments don't function. . . . There is an inertia that . . . creeps over everything like an incoming tide." Capitalists, souring on Harrison, turned to the Democrats as "the party of business." Although the President was renominated in 1892, it was certain that he would be opposing Cleveland without the machine's power and money. As a droll observer of that campaign wryly noted, "each side would have been glad to defeat the other if it could do so without electing its own candidate." But Harrison had had enough. Approached in 1896 to run again, he echoed many a predecessor: "Why should a man seek that which to him would be a calamity?"

ROBERT CUNNINGHAM COLLECTION

Harrison's term saw over five million acres in Oklahoma opened to settlers, and the rushes were usually chaotic. One protested eviction in 1889 (above) forced a local claims arbitration board to resign. In the 1892 cartoon at right Harrison is depicted as too small to wear his grandfather's hat. Boss James Blaine, Harrison's Secretary of State, perched atop a bust of William Henry, croaks "Nevermore," scuttling Harrison's re-election hopes.

Puck

FACTS IN SUMMARY: BENJAMIN HARRISON

CHRONOLOGY

UNITED STATES		HARRISON
	1833	*Born August 20*
Rise of Whig party	1834	
Van Buren elected President	1836	
William Henry Harrison elected President	1840	
Tyler becomes President	1841	
Polk elected President	1844	
Annexation of Texas	1845	
War with Mexico begins	1846	
Battle of Buena Vista	1847	*Enters Farmers' College*
Treaty of Guadalupe Hidalgo	1848	
Taylor elected President		
Fillmore becomes President	1850	*Enters Miami University in Ohio*
Compromise of 1850		
Pierce elected President	1852	*Graduates from Miami University*
Gadsden Purchase	1853	*Marries Caroline Scott*
Kansas-Nebraska Act	1854	*Admitted to the bar*
		Moves to Indianapolis
	1855	*Becomes law partner of William Wallace*
		Becomes notary public
		Appointed commissioner for the court of claims
Buchanan elected President	1856	*Joins Republican party*
Dred Scott decision	1857	*Elected city attorney*
Lincoln-Douglas debates	1858	
John Brown's raid at Harpers Ferry	1859	
Lincoln elected President	1860	*Elected state supreme court reporter*
South Carolina secedes		
Fort Sumter fired upon	1861	*Forms law firm with William Fishback*
First Battle of Bull Run		*Appointed elder of Presbyterian Church*
Battle of Shiloh	1862	*Commissioned second lieutenant*
Battle of Antietam		
Battle of Fredericksburg		*Promoted to captain*
		Commissioned a colonel
Emancipation Proclamation	1863	
Battle of Chancellorsville		
Gettysburg Campaign		
Sherman's march to the sea	1864	*Fights at Nashville*
Battle of Nashville		
Lee surrenders	1865	*Promoted to brigadier general*
Lincoln assassinated		
Thirteenth Amendment ratified		
	1867	*Returns to law practice*

UNITED STATES March 4, 1889 – March 4, 1893

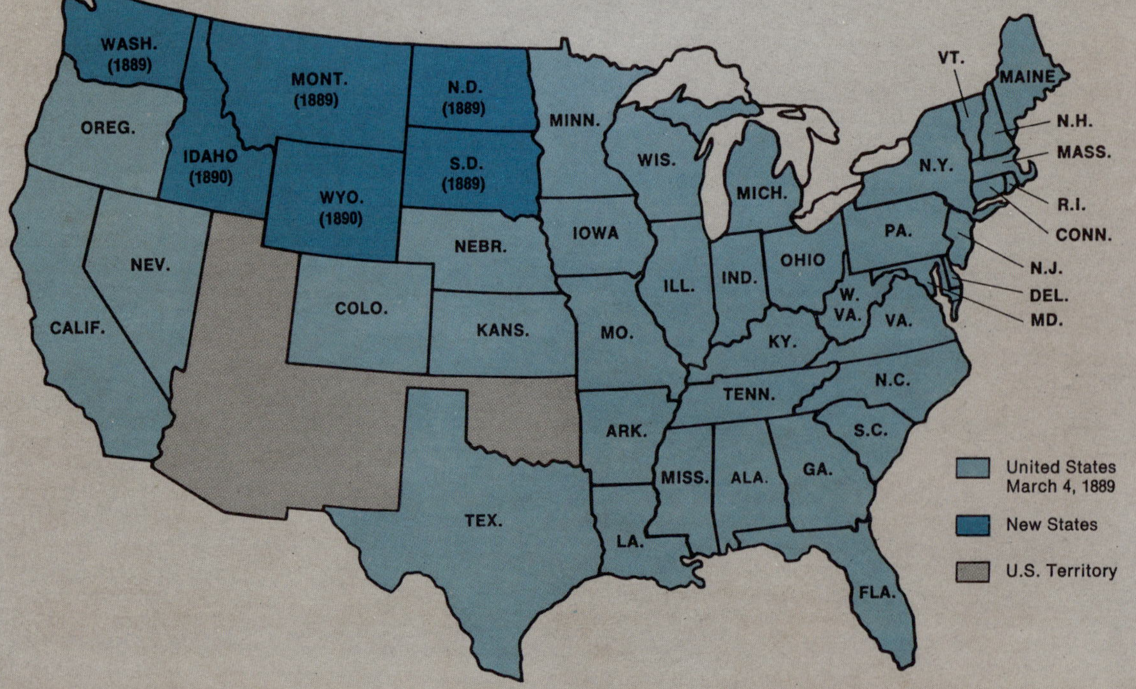

Johnson impeached	1868	
Grant elected President		
Grant re-elected	1872	
	1876	*Loses gubernatorial race*
Hayes elected President	1877	
Bland-Allison Act	1878	
Garfield elected President	1880	
Arthur becomes President	1881	*Elected U.S. senator*
Pendleton Act	1883	
Cleveland elected President	1884	
	1886	*Defeated in bid for re-election*
	1888	*Elected President*
Omnibus bill	1889	
Dependent Pension Act	1890	
Sherman Antitrust Act		
Sherman Silver-Purchase Act		
Cleveland elected President	1892	*Asks Congress to declare war on Chile*
		Caroline Harrison dies
		Defeated in bid for re-election
Cleveland withdraws Hawaii annexation treaty	1893	*Sends Senate treaty annexing Hawaii*
		Returns to Indianapolis
McKinley elected President	1896	*Marries Mary Dimmick*
	1901	*Dies March 13*

BIOGRAPHICAL FACTS

BIRTH: North Bend, Ohio, Aug. 20, 1833

ANCESTRY: English-Scotch

FATHER: John Scott Harrison; b. Vincennes, Ind., Oct. 4, 1804; d. North Bend, Ohio, May 25, 1878

FATHER'S OCCUPATIONS: Farmer; U.S. congressman

MOTHER: Elizabeth Irwin Harrison; b. Mercersburg, Pa., July 18, 1810; d. Aug. 15, 1850

BROTHERS: Archibald Irwin (1832–1870); Carter Bassett (1840–1905); John Scott, Jr. (1844–1926); James Friedlay (1847–1848); James Irwin (1849–1850)

SISTERS: Mary Jane Irwin (1835–1867); Anna Symmes (1842–1926)

HALF SISTERS: Elizabeth Short (1825–1904); Sarah Lucretia (1829–?)

FIRST WIFE: Caroline ("Carrie") Scott; b. Oxford, Ohio, Oct. 1, 1832; d. Washington, D.C., Oct. 25, 1892

FIRST MARRIAGE: Oxford, Ohio, Oct. 20, 1853

SECOND WIFE: Mary Scott Lord Dimmick; b. Honesdale, Pa., April 30, 1858; d. New York, N.Y., Jan. 5, 1948

SECOND MARRIAGE: New York, N.Y., April 6, 1896

CHILDREN: Russell Benjamin (1854–1936); Mary Scott (1858–1930); Elizabeth (1898–1955)

EDUCATION: Private tutoring; attended Farmers' College; graduated (B.A. 1852) from Miami University

HOME: Indianapolis, Indiana

RELIGIOUS AFFILIATION: Presbyterian

OCCUPATIONS BEFORE PRESIDENCY: Lawyer; notary public; soldier

MILITARY SERVICE: Appointed col. in 70th Indiana Volunteers (1862); resigned as brevet brig. gen. in 1865

PRE-PRESIDENTIAL OFFICES: Commissioner for the Court of Claims; City Attorney; Secretary of Indiana Republican Central Committee; State Supreme Court Reporter; Member of U.S. Senate

POLITICAL PARTY: Republican

AGE AT INAUGURATION: 55

OCCUPATION AFTER PRESIDENCY: Lawyer

DEATH: Indianapolis, Ind., March 13, 1901

PLACE OF BURIAL: Crown Hill Cemetery, Indianapolis, Indiana

ELECTION OF 1888

CANDIDATES	ELECTORAL VOTE	POPULAR VOTE
Benjamin Harrison Republican	233	5,447,129
Grover Cleveland Democratic	168	5,537,857
Clinton B. Fisk Prohibition	—	249,506

THE HARRISON ADMINISTRATION

INAUGURATION: March 4, 1889; the Capitol, Washington, D.C.

VICE PRESIDENT: Levi P. Morton

SECRETARY OF STATE: James G. Blaine; John W. Foster (from June 29, 1892)

SECRETARY OF THE TREASURY: William Windom; Charles Foster (from Feb. 24, 1891)

SECRETARY OF WAR: Redfield Proctor; Stephen B. Elkins (from Dec. 24, 1901)

ATTORNEY GENERAL: William H. H. Miller

POSTMASTER GENERAL: John Wanamaker

SECRETARY OF THE NAVY: Benjamin F. Tracy

SECRETARY OF THE INTERIOR: John W. Noble

SECRETARY OF AGRICULTURE: Jeremiah M. Rusk

SUPREME COURT APPOINTMENTS: David J. Brewer (1889); Henry B. Brown (1890); George Shiras, Jr. (1892); Howell E. Jackson (1893)

51st CONGRESS (March 4, 1889–March 4, 1891):
Senate: 39 Republicans; 37 Democrats
House: 166 Republicans; 159 Democrats

52nd CONGRESS (March 4, 1891–March 4, 1893):
Senate: 47 Republicans; 39 Democrats; 2 Others
House: 235 Democrats; 88 Republicans; 9 Others

STATES ADMITTED: North Dakota, South Dakota, Montana, Washington (all 1889); Idaho, Wyoming (both 1890)

PEOPLES' ENTRANCE.
CLOSED
THIS IS
OF THE MON
BY THE
FOR
ENVELOPE TRUST
PAPER BAG TRUST
COAL
TIN TRUST
SUGAR TRUST.
IRON TRUS
STAN TRU